Advance Praise for
Our Savior Our Sisters Ourselves

*In many respects, writing a book is very similar to the birthing process.
Rev. Dr. Jo Ann Browning's first book, "Our Savior, Our Sisters,
Ourselves: Biblical Teachings & Reflections on Women's Relationships,"
is proof that the most beautifully written works are born from the
most wrenching labor! You have been a midwife for so many.
Congratulations on your own, long overdue birth!*

REV. DR. CLAUDETTE ANDERSON COPELAND
Pastor, New Creation Christian Fellowship
San Antonio, Texas

*Having ministered to women for almost 25 years, the Rev. Dr. Jo Ann
Browning has a sensitivity to and compassion for the needs of women
that is not easily rivaled. I have witnessed it from afar and personally
as a sister-friend over the last 10 years. You will experience it in powerful and poignant ways in her first book, "Our Savior, Our Sisters,
Ourselves: Biblical Teachings & Reflections on Women's Relationships."*

REV. DR. CYNTHIA L. HALE
Senior Pastor, Ray of Hope Christian Church

*Rev. Dr. Jo Ann Browning is one of the most outstanding women in
Christendom and it goes without saying that her first book reflects her
profound wisdom, scholarship, and spiritual insight. I appreciate
her willingness to share her best with the sisters of the kingdom, and
I applaud her for giving us a work that will change lives and build
faith. Rev. Jo Ann is a woman after God's heart and she is, indeed, a
friend dear to my heart.*

REV. DR. ELAINE FLAKE
Co-Pastor, The Greater Allen Cathedral of New York

For years I have been waiting for Rev. Dr. Jo Ann Browning to share her insight and wisdom with the women of God. For decades I have watched her minister to and care for women. She has changed women's lives through her retreats, revivals, bibles studies, and more. Now women will have the opportunity to experience her at another level. This book is what is needed for this season.

REV. DR. JESSICA KENDALL INGRAM
Episcopal Supervisor
10th Episcopal District, A.M.E. Church

In her first book, "Our Savior, Our Sisters, Ourselves: Biblical Teachings & Reflections on Women's Relationships," Dr. Jo Ann Browning has published over 25 years of academic and experiential learning. These life lessons are designed to empower, release, and assist women in the fulfillment of their God-given purpose. Her passion and love for the family of God is evident throughout this work. Sisters, I urge you to read, reflect, and be renewed!

REV. DR. BARBARA AUSTIN-LUCAS
Professor, Religious Education & Urban Ministry,
Alliance Theological Seminary; *Founder,* WOMB, Inc.
(Women Organizing, Mobilizing and Building);
and, *Pastor,* Agape Tabernacle International Fellowship,
New York, NY

Our Savior
Our Sisters
Ourselves

Our Savior
Our Sisters
Ourselves

*Biblical Teachings & Reflections on
Women's Relationships*

Rev. Dr. Jo Ann Browning

Journey of Faith
Fort Washington, MD

Our Savior Our Sisters Ourselves
Biblical Teachings & Reflections
on Women's Relationships
By Rev. Dr. Jo Ann Browning

Courtenay S. Brown	Editor & Publisher
Bertha M. Greene	Copy Editor
Circle Graphics	Cover Design & Composition
District Creative Printing Inc.	Printing

Unless otherwise indicated, all scripture quotations are taken from the HOLY BIBLE, NEW INTERNATIONAL VERSION®. Copyright © 1973, 1978, 1984 International Bible Society. Used by permission of Zondervan. All rights reserved.

Scripture quotations marked KJV are taken from the King James Version of the Bible.

Printed in the United States of America
09 08 07 4 3 2

ISBN 978-0-9718553-2-8

Library of Congress Control Number: 2006927605

For further information, please contact:

Journey of Faith
938 E. Swan Creek Road, #264
Fort Washington, MD 20744
drjab@comcast.net
www.drjab.com

Dedication

This book is dedicated to every woman (and woman-to-be) who has impacted my journey of faith and made a difference in my life:

MY GRANDMOTHER
Mary Koontz

MY MOTHER
Ruth S. Leonard

MY DAUGHTER
Candace Jo Ann Mary Browning

MY MOTHER-IN-LAW
Esther A. Browning

MY SISTERS-IN-LAW
Cornelia Browning Moore and Carol Skaggs

MY DAUGHTER-IN-LAW
Courtney Riley Browning

MY GRANDDAUGHTER
Kaylah Jo Ann Browning

Contents

Foreword

If I could describe my mom in one word it would be "amazing." Not only is my mom amazing as a woman of God, but she is amazing at just being my mommy. We have had our ups and downs just like every mother and daughter relationship. There have been times when we just did not see eye to eye, but as I grow older, my mom and I have connected on a different level. Our relationship has different elements that range from teacher to student, friend to friend, and mother to daughter. My mommy knows how to step out of each element and become what I need, whether it is my teacher, friend or mother. As I become a woman and I see all the trials my mom has been through and how she came out of her storms stronger and more powerful, I respect and admire her as an amazing woman of God.

God plays a major role in my life. Growing up in a household of two pastors instilled in me the importance of having a relationship with God. Therefore, it was natural for me to have an understanding of Christianity. Even though God is a part of my life in every way and has been since I was a young child, when I became older, it was hard for me to begin a personal relationship with God, rather than staying in my comfort zone and just believing what my parents told me. I am anticipating the journey to seek God for myself, independent of what my parents taught me. The thought of pursuing my own personal relationship with my Lord and Savior is a great feeling.

God and my role model, my mother, have shaped me into the person I am today. My mommy taught me to trust in God in all things and to always pray and believe that God will see me through anything.

My favorite scripture is John 15: 18-19: "If the world hates you, keep in mind that it hated me first. If you belonged to the world, it would love you as its own. You do not belong to the world but I have chosen you out of the world. That is why the world hates you." This scripture really ministers to me because my mom always told me that I am a "King's kid" and I should carry myself as a "princess." She would say, "Don't be concerned with what other people are doing if it is not of the Lord." Even though I fall short of the glory of God many times, I know I am God's child and I will conduct myself accordingly.

CANDACE JO ANN MARY BROWNING

Preface

For the past 25 years God has used my wife as one of His consecrated and chosen vessels to usher women to a place of international prominence, spiritual position, and Holy Ghost power in the body of Christ. God has miraculously used her to preach to, care for, pray with, love, nurture, and mentor literally hundreds of thousands of women across the world. Her ministry "doth magnify the Lord" and you, the reader, will be profoundly blessed by God's anointing and wisdom that is revealed in these teachings and reflections.

REV. DR. GRAINGER BROWNING, JR.
Senior Pastor, Ebenezer A.M.E. Church

Acknowledgments

I want to thank God for the opportunity to teach and share with the women of Ebenezer A. M. E. Church what was given to me, at various seasons in my life, as I have had the opportunity to serve with my husband, Rev. Dr. Grainger Browning, Jr., Senior Pastor for almost 25 years.

I want to thank God for my husband, who has always encouraged me and insisted, many years ago, that I teach a Bible study that was just for women. Many of those teachings provided the content for this book. I am eternally grateful for my husband's love, support, and encouragement.

I also want to thank God for our son, Grainger III. I have had the awesome privilege as his mother to watch him mature into a shining example of Christian manhood, as a husband and father. His steadfastness has enabled me, in so many ways I can't express them all, to continue on the journey despite some trying and difficult times. He and his wife, Courtney, have blessed us with two beautiful grandchildren, Kaylah Jo Ann and Grainger IV.

I want to thank God for our beautiful, insightful, loving, and strong young adult daughter, Candace Jo Ann Mary, who has demonstrated wisdom beyond her years. She has blessed us with so much joy and happiness and she has taught me so much by the way she has handled life with such inner strength from the God she loves in her heart.

I want to thank God for my beloved mother, Ruth Skaggs Leonard, who when I was a little girl, I likened to a tall, strong, beautiful, brown oak tree. She has always been my earthly strength in good times and in the times of trouble. My mother's love, prayers, encouragement, comfort, and model of Christian womanhood have sustained me and called me back to the things of God when I have strayed.

I want to thank God for my deceased father who always made me think I was the best daughter in the world.

I want to thank God for Daddy Leonard who has always loved and supported everything we have endeavored to do in life.

I want to thank God for my younger brother, Timothy Skaggs, who is a "gentle giant." He and his wife, Carol Baker Skaggs, have always been supportive on the journey.

I want to thank God for my in-laws, Dr. Grainger Browning, Sr., Mrs. Esther Browning, and Elder Cornelia Browning Moore.

I want to thank every Bishop and their wives, the Episcopal Supervisors, that I have been blessed to have the opportunity to serve under: Bishop John H. Adams (retired) and Dr. Dolly Adams, Bishop H. Hartford Brookins (retired) and Rev. Rosalynn Brookins, Bishop Frederick C. James (retired) and Dr. Theresa Gregg James, Bishop Vinton R. Anderson (retired) and Mrs. Vivienne Anderson, and our present Bishop, Adam J. Richardson, Jr. and Mrs. Connie Speight Richardson. I especially want to thank each Episcopal Supervisor for her model of Christian women's leadership.

I want to thank Elder George A. Manning (retired) and his wife Dr. Virginia Manning and my present Presiding Elder Rev. Dr. Louis Charles Harvey for their prayers and support.

I want to thank Presiding Elder Rita Colbert (A.M.E. Zion) for encouraging me to write.

I want to thank my mothers and fathers in ministry; Bishop John R. Bryant and Rev. Dr. Cecelia Williams Bryant, Rev. Dr. William R. Porter and Mrs. Doris A. Porter, and Bishop Corletta Harris Vaughn.

I want to thank the retired Dean of the Divinity School at Howard University, Lawrence Jones, who 25 years ago challenged me to accept the call to the ministry when I could not clearly see my way.

I want to thank Howard Professors Dr. Eugene Rice and Dr. Cain Hope Felder, who encouraged me to pursue my theological education with seriousness, dedication, and excellence.

I want to thank the Pro-Tems of the Ebenezer A. M. E. Church Steward and Trustee Boards, Melvin Clay and Eugene Green, respectively; the Board members; and, the entire Ebenezer A.M.E. Church family for your prayers and support.

I want to thank the women on the ministerial staff who assisted and attended Women to Women Bible Studies. I want to thank every woman who has ever attended Women to Women Bible Studies and the Spiritual Retreat.

I would also like to thank our executive assistants (past and present) for their service: Betty Savoy, Terria Williams, and Katie Bostic.

I want to thank Linda Jones Burns and Dr. Gloria Gibson for their assistance in my previous attempts at writing a book.

I want to thank my circle of beloved sister-friends for your love and prayers.

I want to also especially thank Courtenay S. Brown, my editor and publishing agent, who was used by God. She came forth in a "God Moment" and offered her God-given gifts and talents. I am grateful for her hard work, dedication, and most of all her faith in God that this was the time and the season.

I also want to thank Kim Cassell for her prayers and teaching me how to use the computer to get this book written.

I also want to thank Dr. Sharon Allison Ottey, Trisch Smith, Rev. Kanika Magee, and Rev. Chandra Marriott for reviewing the manuscript before it went to print.

I also want to thank Patricia Smith and Chanika Edwards for transcribing tapes from Women to Women Bible teachings and my handwritten notes.

I would also like to thank Kenneth S. Brown, Esq. and Midgett Parker, Esq. for their legal services and Arnold Williams for his services.

Finally, I sincerely thank God for all of those who have called out my name in prayer as I have tried to do my best on this journey of faith. If I have missed saying thanks to anyone who has helped me on this journey of birthing this book, please charge it to my head and not my heart.

About the Author

Reverend Dr. Jo Ann Browning is co-pastor of Ebenezer African Methodist Episcopal Church in Fort Washington, Maryland. She is married to the Reverend Dr. Grainger Browning, Jr., who is the senior pastor. She is the very proud mother of two children, Grainger III and Candace, and two grandchildren, Kaylah Jo Ann Browning and Grainger Browning IV.

Rev. Dr. Browning graduated from Boston University in 1976 with a Bachelor of Science Degree in Communications. She received a Master of Divinity Degree in 1986 and a Doctorate of Ministry from Howard University School of Divinity in 1991. She was a recipient of the Benjamin E. Mays Fellowship and the Pew Fellowship.

When her husband was appointed to pastor Ebenezer A.M.E. Church in 1983, the church had 17 members and a $12,000 budget. In 1998, Bishop Vinton R. Anderson, presiding prelate of the Second Episcopal District, appointed Rev. Dr. Jo Ann Browning as co-pastor of the Ebenezer A.M.E. Church. This unprecedented appointment officially recognized the Brownings as a pastoral team ministry. In 2006, Ebenezer's membership exceeded 12,000 with more than 100 ministries and a budget exceeding $10 million.

In addition to her responsibilities at Ebenezer, Rev. Dr. Jo Ann Browning has had the opportunity to preach, teach, and facilitate workshops throughout the United States, Haiti, Bermuda, Barbados, Germany, Israel, and South Africa. In July 2002, Rev. Dr. Jo Ann

Browning was inducted into Delta Sigma Theta Sorority, Incorporated as an honorary member. In 2006, she founded Journey of Faith, Inc., a non-profit organization dedicated to empowering women.

Rev. Dr. Jo Ann Browning is grateful for the opportunity to share these teachings that she received from the Lord with all women of God, regardless of race. In all that has been said and done, she continuously gives God all the praise, honor, and glory for the opportunity to be a humble servant of her Lord and Savior Jesus Christ!

Introduction

Ever since I can remember, I have searched for an intimate relationship with God. I wanted to know Him and experience His love for me like I experienced my mother's love and my father's love. In retrospect, I probably searched for that kind of love because my parents got divorced when I was six years old. During my journey of searching and desiring a love relationship with God, I've made many mistakes and substituted His love with the love of others who did not and could not love me. I know for a fact that "can't nobody do you like Jesus!"

The Women to Women Bible Study teachings that have been redacted for this book emerged out of my own journey and my own life experiences. I, too, have gone through some things in my life and I am still going through. My desire is to be in a place in my relationship with God that He will be pleased with everything I do and say. I have fallen short many times, but I keep on trying.

In this book, I have integrated the messages that God gave to me into teachings that explore the reality of being a Black woman, wife, mother, and minister. You may disagree with some of the things I've written, or you may identify with every word you read in this book. It is my sincere prayer that you will discover something within these pages that will resonate with you, empower you, and bless you as you continue on your own journey of faith. I pray that you will always take time to reflect on your life experiences and use what you learn to grow in the things of God.

Life is a journey of faith, and my prayer is that we all embrace the fact that God is "OUR SAVIOR," that we are connected to "OUR SISTERS," and we must love and celebrate "OURSELVES." As you read this book, I implore you to use it as it was intended. I pray that you will "Reflect," then take "Action," and then "Pray" that your relationship with God will grow stronger, and your relationships with others will be closer, and that you will begin to see yourself as the woman who God ordained you to be.

May we all strive for Him to be pleased with our individual journey as we walk in faith.

PART ONE

Our Savior ⚬

1

Pursuing God's Purpose for Your Life

The woman said to him, "Sir, give me this water so that I won't get thirsty and have to keep coming here to draw water."

Then, leaving her water jar, the woman went back to the town and said to the people, "Come, see a man who told me everything I ever did. Could this be the Christ?"

Many of the Samaritans from that town believed in him because of the woman's testimony, "He told me everything I ever did."

(JOHN 4:15, 28-29, 39)

My sisters, have you ever asked yourself: What is my purpose in life? What are God's plans for me? In order to realize God's plans and purpose for your life, you must be involved in an intimate relationship with Him through His Son, Jesus Christ. To enter into a right relationship with God, you must accept Jesus Christ as your Lord and Savior. The closer we draw to God, the clearer and easier it is for us to walk in our purpose. In the *Purpose Driven Life*, Rick Warren writes "without God, life has no purpose and without purpose, life has no meaning and without meaning, life has no significance or hope." Our relationship with God through Jesus Christ is the key to our finding, pursuing, and pressing toward our purpose.

There is a flip side to this pursuit of our purpose. The enemy does not want you to find your purpose. When we are walking in our purpose we are collectively representing God's kingdom on earth, God's glorification, and God's power over evil. So if the enemy can detain and distract you, or convince you that you are "off purpose," or trick you, or slow you down, or frustrate you, he will. The enemy will do anything to stop you in your tracks and keep you from pursuing your purpose. The evil one is a trickster. If you're not careful, before you know it, you'll be collaborating with him. You'll start thinking to yourself:

+ I'm not smart enough.
+ I'm not good enough.
+ The timing is not right.
+ I don't know if I can do it.

All of these negative thoughts directly contradict what God is telling you. When you let negative thoughts crowd your mind and prevent you from pursuing your purpose, you are collaborating with the evil one without even realizing it.

For example, maybe you decided to join a ministry. You went to the first meeting, got all of the material, signed up to work on a sub-committee that night, you went home, and you haven't been to another meeting since. Some of you will not go back to school and get that degree that God told you to get since 1921. It's not money that is stopping you. It is fear that has you bound. My sisters, God has not given us the spirit of fear, but of power, love, and a sound mind. The evil one has convinced you that you don't have what it takes to pursue God's purpose for your life. God did not create us in His image for us to live an unfulfilled life.

Some of us have backed up from our purpose because those closest to us have discouraged us. We have to be clear about our purpose. We have to tell the naysayers in our lives that we are going to be obedient to God with or without their support. If you do what God tells you to do, you'll be better for it. In fact, you'll be better at everything that you do in life because when you are living in your purpose you'll be happy. That is why as we seek God for our purpose, we may need to reflect on our passions and figure out how we can merge them with our gifts and talents to live a more fulfilled life.

As you pursue your purpose in the kingdom you will come up against obstacles, but you must not let them steer you off course. When you find yourself facing an obstacle, you must not throw in the towel or throw your hands up in defeat. There is only one thing you can do when you are faced with an obstacle that has the potential to prevent you from reaching your purpose: You must push harder.

If you don't handle your obstacles, they can cause you to become angry, bitter, and frustrated. If you don't push through your obstacles, as time passes you will look up one day and find that your life has been unrewarding because you never pursued your purpose. My sisters, as long as you are still breathing, it is never too late to pursue your purpose.

Sometimes we are so eager to step into our purpose that we miss the fact that we must be prepared to receive it. God will use the thing that bothers you the most, or the thing that scares you the most, to prepare you for your ultimate purpose. There is a correlation between what you are doing now and your ultimate purpose. When I was struggling with accepting the call to preach, the Lord brought my own time of preparation to my remembrance. When I was in the eighth grade, my mother and my teacher forced me to participate in an oratorical contest. I hated to speak in front of people. The mere thought of public speaking gave me diarrhea. Long story short, I ended up winning first prize. A public speaker was born. I had no idea then that God was preparing me to speak before thousands of people as a pastor. So, don't get frustrated and get off track while God is connecting the dots. Stay on track.

When I think of women who lived out their purpose in the Kingdom of God, Harriet Tubman instantly comes to mind. Catherine Clinton wrote a phenomenal book, *Harriet Tubman: The Road to Freedom* that chronicles Tubman's life. Clinton writes, "Growing from a girl into a young woman, Araminta, [which was Harriet's given name] experienced an intensification of her Christian faith. A deep and abiding spiritual foundation that remained with her throughout her life."

Clinton further states, "It was remarkable that Tubman was willing to travel back into Maryland and even to Baltimore, a notoriously dangerous city for fugitives; any black traveling by boat, train or any public transportation was required to present free papers for inspection. Whether she had obtained forged papers or not, Baltimore remained a risk and unknown environment for Harriet. Perhaps her months in Philadelphia imbued her with confidence about her abilities. It was still a great leap of faith for Tubman to venture into a new city, the first of many on her road to freedom."

When I think of how Harriet Tubman allowed God to use her to lead His people out of slavery, I am simply awestruck by her obedience. Though she was plagued by sickness in her body and was prone to fainting spells as a result of a childhood trauma, she had the strength of ten men. She had an innate sense of determination and fortitude that allowed her to carry out her purpose.

She had obstacles all around her. Her life was threatened every day that she lived. Yet she went back and forth on the Underground Railroad 19 times and led 300 slaves to freedom. She refused to give up! As a result, she is one of the most incredible women in history.

Harriet Tubman was living out her purpose. In her book, Catherine Clinton insightfully asked how Harriet Tubman, "who in a movement dominated by white northern males to free slaves, once a former slave; how did she become both an abductor for the underground railroad and a champion of the radical wing of the abolitionist crusade?" I can answer that question: Her purpose was shaped by her situation. The circumstances of her enslavement and the crippling racism of the day were no match for her Christian faith. Her faith propelled her through those obstacles and towards her purpose.

But here is the truly amazing thing about Harriet Tubman. In 1849, she began a lengthy prayer vigil for the soul of her master! Catherine Clinton writes, "to best fulfill her destiny, her purpose, Tubman realized she must actively seek a role in God's plan rather than letting others dictate her path." Clinton further states that Tubman knew she needed to combine faith with action. Sister Harriet was driven. God gave her what she needed to overcome her obstacles and pursue her purpose because she was obedient.

My sisters, I want you to reflect on another woman who lived out her purpose in life. I call her "the first evangelist of Samaria." She was a loose woman; she was a Samaritan woman; she was a lonely woman; she was a barren woman; and she was a woman who was disrespected in her community. Although she was a sinful woman, she was a knowledgeable woman. You can tell that she knew the Word based on her interaction with Jesus. She was an intelligent woman, but she had no purpose. However, through her encounter with Jesus, she found her purpose. Her purpose was to evangelize.

John 4:4 states that Jesus had to go to Samaria. My sisters, the Lord will do what He needs to do to get your attention. When you are obediently pursuing your purpose, every obstacle you face will ultimately end up benefiting and blessing your purpose. It will not be easy, but when your life is lined up with God's will, you will always be victorious.

Don't be afraid of the process as you pursue your purpose. In fact, you should rest in the process. The woman at the well, like Harriet Tubman, was going through a process in order to fulfill her purpose. The Samaritan woman did not resist engaging Jesus, even though He was a Jew, and Jews did not interact with Samaritans. In John 4:10 Jesus says, "If you knew the gift of God and Who it is that asks you for a drink, you would have asked Him and He would have given you living water."

In John 4:11 the Samaritan woman stepped in and questioned what was being said. This is a key step towards finding your purpose in life. In the process of pursuing your purpose, in the uncomfortable times, in the unknowing times, you must activate your faith in God through Jesus Christ. My sisters, if you take a leap of faith in the process, if you trust Jesus in the process, what you have desired on the inside, you will get for a lifetime on the outside.

Without hesitation, the Samaritan woman tells Jesus to give her the water, so that she will not have to keep coming back. Metaphorically, we all thirst to find our purpose, to find peace and gratification, to find our place in the world, and to find what God created us to do. All of us want to be at peace on the inside. The Samaritan woman was willing to admit what she wanted and what she needed.

Then it happens—Jesus responds to the Samaritan woman by exposing all of her mess. My sisters, don't be afraid of being exposed by God. Sometimes, He has to expose our issues in order for us to move on. Jesus couldn't let the Samaritan woman step into her purpose until she was exposed. Because once she was exposed, then she could be delivered. Jesus had to deliver her from her personal demons before she could step into her purpose.

Some of us will never step into our purpose because we will not let the Lord deliver us. Some of us refuse to acknowledge that we have personal demons. Some of us have already been delivered and we've stepped back into the mess. My sisters, be willing to admit your wrongdoings in pursuit of fulfilling your purpose. Women of God, like the Samaritan woman, you have to want to change. You have to want to move forward.

To begin to fulfill your purpose, you must recognize the hand of God in your life and you must know Jesus for yourself. Like the Samaritan woman you must be willing to recognize that your purpose is intertwined with your relationship with God through Jesus Christ. You have to know God's voice, so that you can recognize Him when He speaks in the midst of your pursuit. If you know Him, then you know His voice. If you know His voice, He will tell you how to make it through to your purpose. When God is telling you what to do, then you—like the Samaritan woman—can move forward with power and confidence. Eventually the Samaritan woman returned to Samaria and told the people about her experience at the well and souls were saved. She became the first evangelist of Samaria.

So, what about your purpose? What is God calling you to do and why haven't you moved forward? God is calling women into their purpose. But there are some things we need to do to get to where He would have us to go. Some of us need to ask for forgiveness. Some of us need to separate ourselves from ungodly people, places, and things. God is calling you to His purpose and now is the time for you to press toward your purpose. He is calling you!

It's time to get on track. It's time for you to reclaim the purpose that God has for you. When we don't diligently pursue our purpose, when we live contradictory lives, when we remain stuck and stagnant, when we won't do what God wants us to do, we grieve God.

My sisters, we need to commit in faith that from this day forward we will pursue our purpose. If we take the first step, God will do the rest. He will put it in motion. He will give you provision. But you must be prepared to receive the provision. It's time that we use our gifts and talents to serve God and His people. That's all that God wants us to do. The enemy would have you think that you're not worthy to serve God. That is a lie from the pit of hell.

God loves us so much more than we realize. When we think about all that God has done for us, we should feel compelled to fulfill our purpose. The Scriptures provide shining examples of women who pursued their purposes: Mary, Miriam, Vashti, Mary Magdalene, Ruth, Esther, Naomi, Hannah, Hagar, Elisabeth, Sarah, the woman with the alabaster box, and the bent-over woman, just to name a few. They honored and blessed God by living out their purpose. He's calling me! He's calling you! He's calling us! Will you be faithful to that which God has called you to do? What are you going to do now? He's calling you.

Reflections in Action

+ Reclaim your God-given reality: You were created woman in the image of God to be blessed. Reclaim it, in case you forgot it. Keep it in the forefront of your mind.

+ Know within yourself that whatever you set out to do or whatever you are doing right now, if it is God's purpose for your life, you shall succeed.

+ As you pursue your purpose or as you live out your purpose, you must have a serious, consistent prayer life.

+ Learn how to connect the dots. You may be doing something right now that might not be your ultimate purpose. However, if you look closely, you will see that it is related to your ultimate purpose in life.

+ Think about your passions. You may find that your purpose is directly linked to those things that you are passionate about.

+ Don't collaborate with the enemy.

+ There will always be obstacles in pursuit and preparation of your purpose. Don't be discouraged.

+ If you know that you have a "giving-up spirit," decide to press forward anyhow.

+ Seek God's supernatural power to strengthen you as you pursue, prepare for, and press toward your purpose.

+ You must approach your purpose with a servant's heart. If you're too focused on personal gain, then you are pursuing your purpose for you, not God's purpose for you.

+ When you are working in your God-given purpose, you should have a sense of inner peace and great joy. If you are doing something that you feel God is calling you to do and you don't have joy—something is wrong. If you have no peace or joy, you are in the wrong place, doing the wrong thing, or the devil is in control.

✦ In pursuit of your purpose, particularly in the church, don't put your mouth on someone else's purpose. If you do, you will have stopped the move of God on your own purpose. Ask God for forgiveness and repent for your wrongdoing, because in order to pursue your purpose, you must have a clean heart.

✦ If you have gotten off track or if you are unsure of your purpose, ask God to give you some answers. Don't be afraid to step into your purpose.

Reflective Prayer

Father God,

Your work is all divine. I thank you for all the work you have done on me and through me. I truly desire to pursue my purpose to your honor and your glory. I thank you dear Lord that you know my heart, you know my desires, and you know your plans for my future.

I will keep on pressing to reach the place where you want me to be. I have made mistakes. I have done and said the wrong things at times in my life. I have gotten off track. I thank you that I can hear your voice when you call me back on track. I pray that all of the women of God will answer when you call them to their purpose.

I bless your name as I walk in the authority you have bestowed on me. I ask you God for your blessings, your guidance, and your supernatural power as I pursue my purpose in life. Grant me the clarity to recognize that you are preparing me to step into the fullness of my purpose. I pray that you grant me the steadfastness and the fortitude to not turn back.

Lord, please strengthen me in my weak places, heal me in my broken places, and deliver me from my sinful nature. Where there is fear Lord, I ask that you replace it with power, love, and a sound mind. Knowing the depth of your love for me, there is no way I want to cause you grief by being stubborn or disobedient.

I love you and I thank you for sending your best to me, Jesus the Christ. And so, I commit to giving my best to you. I commit myself to the building of your kingdom on earth as it is in Heaven. Lord, thank you for giving me a purpose. In Jesus' name I say thank you. In Jesus' name I pray.

Amen.

2

Let Go and Let God

Cast all your anxiety on him because he cares for you.

(1 PETER 5:7)

Casting all your care upon him; for he careth for you.

(KJV)

My sisters, have you ever found yourself in a tight situation wherein your only two choices were either to die or to survive? Maybe your situation was not that extreme. Your two decisions might have been leave or stay, quit or continue, or sink or swim. Whenever I find myself in a situation that makes me question if I have the strength to endure, I find myself reflecting on the strength and courage of my African ancestors—those brave strong men and women who arrived in the United States in the bowels of slave ships. Imagine how tight their situation must have been. They were lying in the dark, dank pit of a slave ship. They were squeezed into cramped, tight spaces that were full of urine and fecal matter on a journey to the unknown.

Think about the women on those ships. Imagine yourselves on those ships. Some of the women were in the beginning stages of pregnancy due to rape. The Portuguese soldiers would identify women who had the strongest bodies to breed children. Those women would then be raped. Some women even gave birth on those dreadful ships. They lay shackled together on those brutal ships, separated from their families and their loved ones. An estimated ten million Africans were enslaved in the Atlantic slave trade over a period of almost four centuries. The new world order that they had been brought into was designed to eliminate all forms and systems of African culture that unified them in order to prevent resistance and rebellion. The slave traders started breaking our ancestors down before they got on the ship, so that when they reached America they would not rebel. The destruction of the African culture was intentional and it was deliberate. The truth is African-Americans are still working through what was done to our ancestors.

My focus is African-Americans because that is who I am. But this discourse has universal applications. Every race, religion, and culture has its own story to tell regarding how its ancestors survived and thrived in the face of depravation and inhumanity. God does sit high and look low, and He holds all of His people in the very palm of His hand. So all of us, Latinas, Asians, Caucasians, African-Americans, and Jews, as women of God, must ask ourselves, "How in the world did our ancestors make it? How in the world did they survive the inhumanness of the day? How did our ancestors maintain their sanity, save their souls, and protect their spirits?"

The answers may be different across cultures, but the fact that the human spirit can rise above the physical condition resonates with us all. In many African societies there was a belief in a supreme creator. Most of our ancestors had faith in a god. The African culture had a frame of reference of an almighty omnipresent God. This frame of reference became the faith foundation and launching pad for the Christian faith that kept and sustained African-Americans from slave ships; through plantations; through the Civil War; through Jim Crow laws; through the industrial revolution; through the civil rights movement; through the technological era, and through racism, classism, sexism and every form of economic, political, and social oppression.

African American history is replete with women who survived their circumstances: Sojourner Truth, Harriet Tubman, Fannie Lou Hamer, Mary McLeod Bethune, Amanda Berry Smith, Rosa Parks, Dorothy Height, and Jarena Lee, to name a few. Jarena Lee, the first licensed, female preacher in the African Methodist Episcopal Church, was an unordained pulpiteer who traveled 2,325 miles and delivered 178 sermons. In 1809, she was attending a worship service. When the white United Methodist preacher got up to preach, something happened to his tongue. It had cleaved to the roof of his mouth. The Holy Ghost pushed Jarena Lee up and she started preaching from the pew. After witnessing her sermon, Bishop Richard Allen, who had originally denied her request to preach, apologized to her. He realized that she was indeed called by God.

Women have always had to go through trials to get to where God called us to be. We've always had to go through something to get to what God has for us. How did our sisters make it on the slave ships? How were they able to overcome their trials so that we can keep on going today? What was it about the women in all of our families who had so much less and yet they did so much more? They made it through because they knew how to give their troubles to God. Simply put, they understood one of the most fundamental Christian principles: Let go and let God.

We say it all the time. It has become a Christian catch phrase of sorts: Let go and let God. It is time that we learn what it really means to give everything over to God. It's time that we learn how to give it all to God and pray. In other words, stop trying to help God solve your problems. God is all powerful. He does not need our assistance.

My sisters, we need to stop trying to control our own destinies. We need to put everything in God's hands: Let go and let God. We only end up stressing ourselves out when we try to fix things on our own. When we get in God's way we end up miserable. There are some things in life that we have to let God work out for us.

I don't want you to think that it's any easier for me to let go and let God because I am a preacher of the Gospel. For example, I once visited a wonderful spa. (As women, it is very important that we regularly take time out for ourselves.) I had an absolutely incredible massage. At the end of my 55 minutes, the massage therapist, who had been practicing for 18 years, proceeded to massage my scalp, my temples, and my jaw. She said, "You have a lot of things on your mind and you need to relax." And then, as she was finishing up, she whispered to me, "Let go and let God." So you see, regardless of our vocations, we all need help in that area of our lives.

It is absolutely necessary that we embrace this principle of letting go and letting God. It is something that we all must learn to do. Some things are easier to let go than others. We must ask God to give us the gift of discernment, so that we can identify our troubles and give them to God. When we let our problems rule us, they can eat away at our souls and have adverse effects on our well-being. Unresolved trouble manifests itself as high blood pressure, diabetes, and cancer. God is calling for women of faith to actively release their problems and give them to Him.

You know that sick feeling that you get in the pit of your stomach when you're facing trouble? It's that sense of uneasiness that overtakes you when the bill collector calls, or the electric company turns off your lights, or your checkbook reflects a negative balance. You panic and you start to feel physically ill. Your problems begin to constantly annoy, irritate, and nag at you. You can't see a way out of your situation. You start to feel discouraged and you just want to give up. If you're not careful, you can get so bogged down in worrying about your problems that your spirituality begins to suffer. You don't pray with the same fervor. You stop going to church. Slowly but surely, you begin to turn your back on God.

When you find yourself spiritually out-of-sync, then you should know for sure that it's time to release your problems. These are the kinds of problems that God wants you to release to Him. It's foolish to allow ourselves to be held hostage by our problems when God is so willing to resolve them for us. We like to think that we are spiritually mature enough to handle most things, but oftentimes we are not. We need to recognize that God is always able.

Let me break down how the enemy messes with you. The church is one of his favorite places to distract you. If there's something exciting going on in the service, you can stay focused. As long as you're being pumped up and as long as the praise and worship is going on, you can stay focused. As long as the preacher is giving his or her all throughout the sermon, you will be engaged in the message. But if the preacher is making the tithing appeal, or an announcement that you are not interested in, you get distracted, your problems start to creep into the forefront of your mind and you disconnect.

It's just like life. In the quiet moments in your life your thoughts and imagination can run wild and before you know it, you may reconnect with the past and present mess in your life. It is in that moment, if you listen carefully, that God is telling you to give your problems to Him. Give it to God and pray. Let go and let God.

Actively letting go is a process that you may have to repeat a few hundred times, but keep on doing it until your problems no longer have a hold on you, but you have a hold on them. In other words, even though it may not be resolved and the issue is still an issue (that man is still crazy, the boss is still evil, and the case is still in court) you must be able to still have joy and to still have peace in the midst of your troubles.

Peter wrote the First Book of Peter to help Christians endure life's trials. The women on the slave ships knew what Peter was talking about. They had something deep within them on the slave ship. That something blossomed into the full knowledge of God. That knowledge sustained them on the plantations, all across the tobacco and cotton fields, and even in the big house. When our ancestors learned about Jesus they took Him into their hearts and they connected with the Holy Spirit. They held on through the rapes, the abuse, and the loss of loved ones. They held on through uncertain futures. Through it all, they continued to trust and believe in God.

Peter's words resonate for us today as well. They tell us to be encouraged, to endure, and to embrace life's trials and tribulations as opportunities for spiritual growth. The law of Christian serenity is in the Lord, Jesus Christ. Therefore, as Christian women we must learn how to actively cast all our anxieties upon the Lord.

Psalm 55:22 instructs us to, "Cast your burdens upon the Lord." In Matthew 6:34 (KJV) Jesus says, "Take therefore no thought for the morrow: for the morrow shall take thought for the things itself." Or, as the New International Version so succinctly states, "Tomorrow will worry about itself. Each day has enough trouble of its own." My sisters, we cannot worry ourselves sick; instead we must go forth with the confidence and faith that Jesus the Christ will certainly take care of us.

We can be certain with our African-American, Latina, Asian, Jewish, and Caucasian women selves, that because the Lord loves us all, because the Lord calls us all, because the Lord cares for us all, our troubles will not last always. We are not to carry the burdens of our sins any longer. Jesus did that for us on the cross more than two thousand years ago. The things that we must endure in life have not come to break or destroy us, but to make us stronger in the things of God. It is with that divine understanding and blessed assurance that we can overcome any problem that comes our way.

The devil wants us to feel defeated. But we have what it takes to stand the heat, because we know that our change is surely going to come in Jesus. My sisters, if nothing else, we must know that God is in control. We can give it to Him. He can handle it. We can let it go. We can let God work it out on our behalf. We can give it to Him and we can pray. And we can rest assured that all things are working together for good for those who love God and are called according to His purpose.

Who would have ever thought that those women rocking in the slave ship, raped, beaten, pregnant, separated, and enslaved would survive it all and stand? They are still standing. They stand in each and every one of us. We are the walking, living, breathing proof that they survived. It's time that we stand up for them. It's time for us to kick over our stumbling blocks. It's time to let go and let God. It's time to encourage each other.

If you're harboring any ill will or if you are holding a grudge against somebody, I urge you to get rid of it right now. God cannot work on your blocked spirit. Release that negative energy and free yourself up, so that God's Holy Spirit can overtake you. God's got something better for you. Let go and let God. The reason you can't get what God has for you is because you're stuck. Whatever you're stuck on, if it hasn't changed, you need to accept that you do not have the power to change it. So you might as well let it go and let God work it out for you.

If you've been waiting for God to turn something around in your life and it hasn't been turned around yet, the Lord is telling you to give it to Him. He will turn it around. You've been trying to manipulate and massage it to turn it around. You can't do it. God has to do it. He's waiting for you to let it go. Take your hands off of it and watch God fix it for you. Let go and let God. Let go and let God. Let go and let God!

Reflections in Action

- ✦ Write down what you need God to do for you.

- ✦ When you have written it out, put it in the trash.

- ✦ Let go, you can't fix it. You can't do anything about it.

- ✦ Recognize your need to manipulate or control certain situations in your life, and release those situations to God.

- ✦ Acknowledge the times when you have (willingly or unwillingly) interrupted God's plan for your life, and ask God to forgive you.

- ✦ Identify the reasons why it is so difficult for you to let go and seek God's help.

- ✦ Take the time to reflect on why you are still going places that you know you should not go, or why you are still involved with people who you know are preventing you from being the woman God created you to be.

- ✦ Realize that there are limits to your ability to affect change in certain situations in your life, and stop wasting your energy trying to fix things that are out of your control.

- ✦ Embrace the reality of the infinite power of God in all areas of your life.

Reflective Prayer

Father God,

In the name of Jesus I say thank you. Thank you for being a balm in Gilead for the sin-sick soul. Thank you for being a balm in Gilead when I am discouraged and drowning in despair. Thank you for being a balm in Gilead just when I wanted to give up and give in.

Father God, I thank you that you have told me to "Let go and let God." Lord God, when I say those words I feel lighter, I feel better, I feel affirmed, I feel confirmed, I feel convicted, and I feel assured. I am confident in you.

Father God, you do all things well. I thank you in the midst of my struggles. I trust that these trials and tribulations have come to make me stronger. God, enter my heart and let me feel your awesome power.

Lord, I thank you for the breakthrough. I thank you that you walk with me. I thank you for the fact that you are always nearby. I thank you and I praise you for the fact that you are so willing to fight my battles. Therefore, I know deep down in my sanctified soul that everything is going to be alright.

Lord, I thank you for the revelation that you are in control in all things, and I do not have to burden myself with unresolved problems and concerns. I realize that you have the ultimate power to take care of all things. I embrace the power of Jesus the Christ.

Now God bless me and seal everything with your Holy Ghost. In Jesus' name I commit myself to letting go and letting God. In Jesus' name I pray.

Amen.

3

It's the Least We Can Do

I beseech you therefore, brethren, by the mercies of God, that ye present your bodies a living sacrifice, holy, acceptable unto God, which is your reasonable service.

And be not conformed to this world: but be ye transformed by the renewing of your mind, that ye may prove what is that good, and acceptable, and perfect, will of God.

ROMANS 12:1-2 (KJV)

My sisters, it's time for a change. A change of view, that is. Have you ever realized that some things have become so familiar that you can't see the point in revisiting them? Consider the scriptures. Some of us know certain scriptures so well that we can quote them as easily as we say our names. But, sometimes, though we speak the Word, we tend to lose sight of its power.

Sometimes when we review those familiar scriptures, God gives us a deeper insight and revelation. In other words, sometimes God will send us back to that scripture that we can quote up one side and down the other and show us something brand new. My sisters, we must be careful about falling into a spiritual routine. You attend Sunday services every week. The enemy wants you to think that it's okay to miss a Sunday every once in a while, because you're familiar with the order of worship, you're familiar with the call to worship, and you're familiar with the doxology. But I guarantee you it will be that very Sunday that you miss, that the Word would have been just for you.

If you pay attention, you will notice that you can always glean a new revelation and a different interpretation of familiar scriptures. That's because the Bible is God's "living Word." So pay attention, seek additional insight in the Word, and God will give you something fresh and new.

Romans 12:12 is a very familiar scripture. In this letter, Paul is challenging Christians to reach for a higher standard. Paul has no qualms in exposing and then addressing what we may not want to admit. The truth is that being a Christian is a daily struggle. The struggle is no different from the pulpit to the pew. If you are not struggling every day, something is wrong. If you think you're above reproach, something is wrong. If you're not in a constant battle to overcome your flesh every day, something is wrong.

If you think you have it all together because you've been saved for 20 or 30 years, or because you speak in tongues, or because God has gifted you, something is wrong. If you think that you are better than somebody else, higher than somebody else, or deeper than somebody else; honey, something is wrong. We all have room to grow. We all struggle with ourselves on a daily basis.

If you think that you are excluded from the struggle—you're fooling yourself. And believe me, if you don't recognize that you are struggling, the enemy has you just where he wants you. If you are convinced that the daily struggle does not apply to you, but you have noticed the following behaviors in yourself, then you may need to check yourself:

+ *You isolate yourself.* If you make it a daily practice to shun other people or exclude others from your life, there's a problem.
+ *You are easily irritated and annoyed.* If everything gets under your skin and you are always unhappy, there's a problem.
+ *You are too deep and profound for the rest of us.* If you think that only you've got the exclusive insight, and that God

speaks only to you, and you're above everybody else, there's a problem. I don't care if you sit in the pulpit or the pew. This word is for everybody. If this is you, there's a problem.

✦ *You know it all.* If you refuse to accept guidance, or constructive criticism, or good counsel because you think you know everything, there's a problem.

✦ *You can't move with God.* If you are unable to adjust to change, you are in a spiritual rut. For example, it took a long time for people to accept me when we were called to pastor Ebenezer A.M.E. Church, because my presence in the pulpit caused a shift. It was something new and different. A woman in the pulpit was not the norm. It was difficult for people to see beyond my gender, but God can move through any vessel He chooses. If you refuse to accept a change for the better, there's a problem.

✦ *You question God.* If you're lined up with the will of God and you're in tune with the spiritual things of God, even though you may not understand them, you can still say, "God, I put my faith and trust in you." But when you question God's will for your life, and then you choose to walk another way because you don't understand God's will, there's a serious problem.

✦ *You are never wrong.* If you can't "woman up" and admit when you are wrong, there's a problem.

✦ *You've lost your sense of compassion.* If you can't be kind-hearted or supportive, there's a problem.

I would dare say, that every woman who reads this chapter will notice that she has exhibited at least one of those behaviors at one time or another. We all need to work on where we are in Christ Jesus. It is time for us to grow up. It is time to come clean with God and release all the mess.

Paul penned practical advice for us in the Book of Romans. Through his writing, Paul is trying to tell us what it takes to live holy. He is giving us a roadmap for the journey ahead. In Romans 12:1 when Paul "beseeches" us to live holy, he is actually referring back to Romans 11.

In Romans 11:25, the Bible says the people of Israel were disobedient and blind. But in 11:26 (KJV) the Bible says, "And so all Israel shall be saved: as it is written, there shall come out of Sion the Deliverer, and shall turn away ungodliness from Jacob." The people were blessed, because of God's covenant with them (Romans 11:27).

God is a God who moves in and through history. Nothing that happens to us in this life will occur without God allowing it to happen. Therefore, nothing is out of God's control. Nothing that has taken place in our lives has happened outside of the will of God. The key to God's covenant with the people of Israel and the key to God's promise to us is written in Romans 11:29 (KJV), "the gifts and calling of God are without repentance." Whatever God has purposed for your life is for His glory. Your gifts are for His glory. Your talents are for His glory. Your gifts have not been given to you to make you look good, or to stroke your ego, or improve your position in the world—it is for God's glory. This means, my sisters, God must be glorified in our lives at all times.

It's time that we elevate our spiritual maturity to the next level. We've got to be able to move with God. We've got to develop some spiritual toughness to harness some things in our natural beings, so that we can be more spiritual. We must move to the place where we are mature enough to admit mistakes and ask God for forgiveness. We can't keep on doing and saying stuff that is not right. We must begin to totally move in the very will of God.

Paul ends Romans 11 with the word "amen," which means let it be so, as if it's the end, as if that's it. But in Romans 12, he goes on to give practical advice based on God's plan in Romans 11. In Romans 12, Paul gives us an addendum to the theological discourse he gave in Romans 11.

Paul begins Romans 12 by beseeching us to act. Beseeching is stronger than just asking someone to do something. By beseeching us, Paul is sending us an earnest and urgent request. If someone beseeches you to act, they essentially are begging, imploring, and appealing to you to act on an urgent matter. I beseech you. Paul is urging the people to live holy out of respect for the fact that God held back His strong hand of judgment from them. The people of Israel had been disobedient and disloyal and God could have wiped them out, but He didn't. Some of you reading this know exactly what I'm writing about.

You know that God should have judged you. You know that God should have wiped you out, but He didn't. Instead, He showed you mercy. Therefore living holy is the least you and I can do.

Paul instructs us how to present our bodies. The body is the temple of the Holy Spirit. It is the instrument by which the Holy Spirit works. As women of God, we must serve Him with our entire being: mind, body, and soul. God works through our bodies and our minds so that our visions can become a reality.

We are to give our bodies as a living sacrifice. As Christians, our living must reflect who we are and whose we are. That means our walk, our talk, and our actions should be a reflection of our faith in God. We must be consistent in how we present ourselves to the world: Don't be pious on Sunday and pissed on Monday.

My sisters, the word of God is saying that you must offer everything you are and everything you do as an act of worship to God. The NIV Bible calls this your "spiritual act of worship." It is your reasonable service. The attitude of serving ought to be a voluntary undertaking. You will experience true worship when you offer yourself to God. We must offer ourselves to God every day, no matter where we are, and no matter what we do. In your working, mothering, sistering, befriending, and loving, in all that you do, offer it all to God.

In order to prepare yourself to offer your "reasonable service to God," you've got to admit that you need to change. You must be transformed by the renewing of your mind. You must make a shift from your old ways to a place where you are grounded. When we are not grounded, we have a tendency to go for the spectacular and sensational. God is not looking for you to be overzealous; He wants you to perform reasonable service. Reasonable service is not joining all 15 choirs or all 100 ministries at your church. That is zealous service. That type of service causes burnout. God is looking for you to be consistent and reasonable in the service that you offer up.

The renewing of your mind entails more than your decision to change. The Greek word for restore is *anakainizo*. *Kainos* is a derivative of the word *neos*, which means new, youthful, fresh, and regenerated. Therefore, my sisters, when you choose to renew your mind, God can regenerate your entire being into something brand new. Old things will have passed away and you will be made brand new.

When we are new beings in Christ, we are to worship God with our total selves every day. That means we have to live holy 24/7. It will not be easy—it will be a struggle. Our flesh is always warring with our spirit. How can we fight our flesh? We can repent for our wrongdoings, and we can have a made up mind that we are in this war to win. Then we must practice those things that are good and acceptable and within the perfect will of God for our lives.

When we are new beings in Christ, we must move out of our places of comfort. We will never, ever be what God wants us to be if we remain comfortable and complacent. We must be consistent and reliable because God is calling us to a new position in life. But some of us have become blindly complacent in our Christian walk. We don't recognize the need for our own renewal. We can see the need for renewal in others, but we can't see it in ourselves. Simply put, if you want to go to where God wants to take you, you have to be willing to change your ways.

Now, some of you are reading this and thinking to yourselves, "I don't smoke, I don't drink, and I don't fornicate, so this does not apply to me." Yes, it does. Because though you might not commit those sins, if you gossip; if you're judgmental; if you're negative; or if you're haughty, puffed up, spiritually arrogant, or inconsistent, then you are not ready to move with God. We cannot glorify God if we've got all this junk in our trunks. We cannot worship Him in spirit and in truth if we are not willing to put forth the effort to change. God cannot be glorified in our lives when we allow our flesh to win.

It's time to take accountability for our past actions, repent, and move on. It's time to seek God's deliverance. Be not conformed to this world, but be ye transformed by the renewing of your mind. God is beseeching us to change. He is beckoning us and He is calling us to another place in Him. God wants us to clean out our spiritual closets. We must get rid of those things that are holding us back. We must make up our minds and commit to change. Think about it. After all God has done for us, it's the least we can do. God sent His only begotten Son to suffer, bleed, and die for us. Therefore, our reasonable service is to strive to be all He wants and desires us to be. It's the least we can do.

Reflections in Action

✦ Ask God to deliver you from your stuff (it's between you and God). If you want God to deliver you, ask Him.

✦ Present your body as a living sacrifice to God. Keep yourself holy and clean.

✦ Be aware of the fact that life will cause you to slip. But God will forgive your slip-ups if you repent.

✦ Once God has delivered you, you must protect your joy— don't let the enemy steal it.

✦ Separate yourself from the people, places, and things that prevent you from offering yourself to God.

✦ Find a way to use your gifts to glorify God.

✦ If you say you'll do it, do it! Be consistent and reliable in your service.

✦ Remember that the Lord loves you in spite of your mess-ups; He forgives you in spite of your mix-ups, so the least you can do is get yourself straight.

✦ Be honest about your shortcomings. Open yourself up and bare your soul to God and be delivered.

✦ The only way to win a war is to have the right weapons— keep your sword (your Word) with you at all times. If you can't keep your Bible in your hand, then keep a hymn in your heart.

✦ Institute prayer time in your daily journey of faith.

Reflective Prayer

Father God,

I want to be in your presence and I want to be obedient to you. God, I realize that it is mandatory for me to continuously check myself out so that I will be in your will and so that I can be a part of the process of building your kingdom on earth as it is in Heaven.

Father God, I realize and I recognize who you are in my life. Lord, every time you give me an opportunity to serve you, I desire that you are pleased. I want everything I do, everything I say, and every move I make to be pleasing in your sight. As I grow a little more in you, I pray that there will be fewer excuses for my actions.

Lord, I want to get to the point where there are no more excuses. You are the only one who is perfect. I want to move as close as I can possibly get to perfection. Lord, I don't know how much longer I may have on this side of Glory, but I do know that however long the time is, I want to get it right. I want to get it right. I must get it right.

You've been so good to me. You've been good to me even when I've been disobedient to you. I thank you Lord for blessing me and keeping me in spite of myself. Thank you for using a familiar word to give me a new revelation. I now know what I have to do. Lord, please forgive me, renew me, invigorate me, regenerate me, refresh me, and direct me to give you the reasonable service that you are due. Quiet the zealous spirit within me that I might be consistent and reliable in the service I perform. I know that in due season, I will reap what I have sown. In Jesus' name I pray.

Amen.

4

Faith
A Foundational Truth

*You need to persevere so that when you have done the will of God,
you will receive what he has promised. For in just a very little while,
"He who is coming will come and will not delay. But my righteous
one will live by faith. And if he shrinks back, I will not be pleased
with him."*

(HEBREWS 10:36-38)

*Now faith is being sure of what we hope for and certain of what we
do not see.*

(HEBREWS 11:1)

My sisters, have you ever doubted that God would do what
He said He would do for you?

Do you always believe in God or do you occasionally question
His ability to fulfill His promises? Do you stick with God or do you
waver in your faith? Did you remain in the faith during that last
trial you faced, or did you back up from your faith? The truth be
told, we all waver in our faith. We all do, even me. All of us, at one
time or another, have let go of our faith in God.

Faith is essential in our journey as Christian women of God. It's
what I call a "foundational truth." It is what we as Christians ought
to stand firm upon. Our faith should be the backbone of our belief

system. Having faith means that you put your trust in God through Jesus Christ no matter what you are facing. Faith allows us to look at our problems, and even though things appear to be one way, our faith reminds us that in due season it shall be another way. That's what faith is—faith is the substance of hope. Faith gives us supernatural vision: it gives us the insight to know that what we may see and experience in the natural shall not always be.

Faith allows us to look at what is wrong and know that ultimately, everything will be alright. My sisters, God has made it clear to me that although we know the power of faith, we do not always activate our faith in all things. Some of us vacillate—one minute we're full of faith and the next minute we're not. We go back and forth. We do not stand firm.

In times of trouble, we even question God's power. We start to wonder whether or not He is able to do what we said He would do. When we really get weak in the faith, and we all do, we even doubt God's ability. We put limitations on God's might. We forget that God is God and that before there was Him there was none other. We forget that God is able to do exceedingly and abundantly above all we can ever think or imagine.

Reality dictates that we will go through some problems in this life. If you're not facing a problem at this moment, just wait a little while. Life has a way of challenging us—and the challenges are constant. They crop up all year long. But no matter what comes our way, we must keep the faith.

- If your husband walks out on you in January, keep the faith.
- If your daughter gets pregnant in February, keep the faith.
- If you get fired in March, keep the faith.
- If you get sick in April, keep the faith.
- If you lose a loved one in May, keep the faith.
- If you lose your home in June, keep the faith.
- If your significant other calls off the wedding in July, keep the faith.
- If you're still not in that relationship that you have been praying for in August, keep the faith.
- If your new business is still failing in September, keep the faith.

✦ If your parents get sick in October, keep the faith.
✦ If your son gets incarcerated in November, keep the faith.
✦ As long as you are still breathing in December, keep the faith!

God never promised us that this life would be easy. But by faith, we can endure all things.

All of us have stepped back from the things of God at one time or another because God did not come through for us when we wanted Him to. But God is calling us to another place. He is calling us to a place of faith where regardless of the time frame, regardless of how massive our problems are, regardless of the setback, we have got to hold on and put our faith and trust in Him.

If we believe that faith is one of the foundational truths, then we need to be so strong in the faith that as the year rolls on, no matter what we are faced with, we will stand firm and not waver. No matter how devastating the situation may be, we have got to hold on to God in faith. The Bible is clear in Hebrews 10:36-38. It tells us that not only must we have faith, but we must persevere in our faith. God is not pleased when He sees us allowing our faith to waver.

The Book of Hebrews gives us the definition of faith. The King James Version of Hebrews 11:1 reads, "Now faith is the substance of things hoped for, the evidence of things not seen."

Theologians agree that Hebrews was probably written by a teacher who may have been afraid that his students were drifting away from the faith. Some theologians believe Paul wrote Hebrews and Luke translated it. There are even some theologians who believe that Aquila and Priscilla, the team ministry from Acts 18:26, may have written it. Only God knows who actually wrote the Book of Hebrews.

Faith is the substance of things hoped for. It is the confident belief that God will come through for you in His time. Faith says it shall come, it shall be:

✦ I will be married.
✦ I will have children.
✦ I will have a home.

+ I will be gainfully employed.
+ I will get my degree.
+ I will get a new car.
+ I will be healthy.
+ I will get a promotion.

Faith says I will. We need to embrace the fact that we serve a God who is able to do anything that we so desire. Faith says: I will, I shall, and I am.

But, my sisters, we must do more than simply "have" faith. We must "activate" our faith. We've got to start expecting God to move. We must reach down into the core of our spirit and activate our faith to the point that we believe that God will do what He said He would do in our lives. Belief is active. We have got to exercise what I call a "now faith" in God. We've got to keep it going all the time. We can't shelve it until we need it. Our faith has to be active all the time, even now, as you read this chapter.

Keep your faith active so that whenever you encounter a difficult situation, your faith kicks in immediately. If you're faced with a potentially overwhelming problem speak faith into it and say, "Now faith! I believe it now."

In other words, there's no need for us to keep complaining about the same old thing over and over. Kick into now faith. Now faith is a faith that is waiting, expecting, and anticipating God to move. Now faith does not shut down because what you want has not come to pass yet. Now faith leaves the door wide open for God. It signals to our Heavenly Father that we are actively waiting for Him to move.

A now faith believes that somehow, someway, sometime it's going to happen. I don't know when, but it doesn't matter because I've got a now faith. I don't know what month, I don't know what day, and I don't know what time, but it shall happen because my faith said now. God is looking down at His daughters from the portals of Heaven. He is looking to see if we have a now faith in Him. So whatever you need from God, your faith has already seen you receiving it.

You don't have to wait for any kind of evidence, you don't have to fake happiness while you wait, and you don't have to conjure it up.

Faith is the substance of things hoped for. Faith is being sure that what we are hoping for is just around the corner. Faith is confidence in God.

Faith allows you to stand boldly against the world. Even if you are suffering, even if there are no apparent solutions, even if your family thinks you are crazy, even if you don't have a penny in your pocket, even if you are unpopular, you must remain in the faith anyhow. You must stand boldly in the spirit of God in the faith.

Faith allows you to speak with certainty because you believe that what God has for you is for you. Faith in God is the supernatural evidence of what you can't see in the natural. You have to believe that although we can't see it and although we can't touch it, it is about to happen. So there's no need for drama. Women of God, we've got to stop putting our energy and time into those things that can't do a thing for us. We've got to look in the mirror, look ourselves in the eyes, get that latest problem in the forefront of our minds, and choose to take a different approach to it.

- ✦ I am not going through any more changes over this problem.
- ✦ I am not losing any more sleep over this problem.
- ✦ I am not popping pills to escape this problem.
- ✦ I am not drinking alcohol to drown this problem.
- ✦ I am not going to sleep around with men to take my mind off this problem.
- ✦ I am not going to slip, slide, sneak, or hide to avoid this problem.
- ✦ I am not going to shoot off at the mouth about this problem.
- ✦ I am not going to try to prove that I can handle this problem on my own.
- ✦ I am not going to argue with anybody else about this problem.
- ✦ I am fine, because I know that the Lord is going to work this problem out for me.

Then sit back, cross your legs, and activate your faith and watch God work it out for you.

Faith says the future is not uncertain for us. We serve a God that gives us a certain future. We are in His hands. Our lives are in His hands. Therefore, we don't have to worry about anything. Stop worrying about this and that. Stop worrying about your husband, your children, and your job. Give yourself to God, put your faith in Him and watch His hand be steady.

When God makes you a promise, you can believe He will come through for you. And even if He has not spoken to you, even if He's been silent, if you've desired some things in your heart and you've sought the Lord, activate your faith and just wait on Him.

Consider my faith testimony. Pastor Grainger Browning and I have been married for over 20 years. Many of you have heard Pastor tell the story of how we met at the International House of Pancakes. I want to share the story from my perspective.

When we got married in 1979, we moved to Maryland with no job and no job prospects. We lived in a roach-infested apartment on Riggs Road in Hyattsville, Maryland. I had to pound the pavement every day, because initially I was the bread winner while my husband was a full-time seminary student. It took me three months to find a job. During that three-month search, we had no income. Our phone service got disconnected, we were eating scrambled eggs for every meal, and we were about to be evicted.

In the midst of all that, the Lord placed on my husband's heart that we needed to tithe the money from our wedding gifts. We were obedient. We put our faith in God and we watched our already small bank account dwindle down to $50. It didn't look right at the time. I couldn't see how it was going to work out. But remember, faith is the substance of things hoped for and the evidence of things not seen.

The Lord opened the door for me to work at Howard University. They couldn't even call me at home to offer me the job because my phone was disconnected. I had to call them from a 7-11 store to see if I had gotten the job. During my second year of working at Howard, the Lord called me to preach. So, I applied to Boston University's School of Theology.

My husband graduated from seminary and we packed up for Boston. Two weeks before we were supposed to move, the property manager called us to tell us that we did not get the apartment because we were unemployed. But we stayed in the faith and we moved to Boston anyway. We lived with my parents, my in-laws, and my husband's grandparents. We ended up living in a duplex that was owned by an elderly Welsh man who allowed us to live in his house with no references or jobs. We were operating in faith. Within the year, our money was so tight that if we did not live near our parents, we wouldn't have had any food.

Our son, Grainger Browning, III (GT), who was born in July 1981, was still in diapers when we moved back to Massachusetts. I remember leaving the house one morning with GT. I had put the last diaper I had on him and took him to the daycare that we could barely afford. When I came back home that night, I found a huge box of diapers and a card inside the screen door. To this day, I still don't know where it came from. That's how God works. Another day we found an envelope stuffed with $300 in cash and no signature inside the screen door. We didn't even know who to thank. Every time we got down to the wire, God would break through for us.

My husband never did get a job. He'd always be one of three finalists, but he never got the job. So he started substitute teaching for $35 a day. One day he got hit in the eye with a ball during recess. The school nurse told him to go home. He said, "I can't go home, I need this $35." The nurse assured him he would be paid and he came home to rest his bruised eye. Within five minutes of his arrival home, John Hurst Adams, who was the bishop of the Second Episcopal District, called and asked if we would come back to Maryland. He wanted my husband to pastor a church called Ebenezer.

Prior to receiving the call from Bishop Adams, I was blessed to become the only seminary student, to my knowledge, to receive a $5000 Benjamin E. Mays fellowship to attend seminary anywhere in the country. My credits easily transferred from the Boston University School of Theology to Howard University's School of Divinity. We left Massachusetts to relocate to Fort Washington, Maryland, only to find out that the parsonage that belonged to Ebenezer had already been rented out.

A week before GT and I arrived permanently in Maryland, our father in ministry, Reverend William R. Porter, found us a townhouse in Southeast DC. The house had urine stains in the carpet, no air conditioner, no hot water, and no screens in the window. But God told us to stay. Faith is the substance of things hoped for, the evidence of things not seen. We had sold all of our furniture except our bedroom sets. We didn't even have a kitchen table. So we all would eat, as a family, at GT's child-sized table. My husband and I would sit sideways and GT would sit with his little legs under the table.

When we finally got into the parsonage, we found out that the septic tank had been backed up for four years. But, through it all we believed in God and we stayed faithful. And then God worked a miracle at Ebenezer A.M.E. Church. We watched Him take 17 members and multiply them over and over and over again. Today, Ebenezer A.M.E. Church is one of the largest A.M.E. churches in the United States. Keep the faith.

I don't know what you need God to do in your life because sometimes it's best not even to identify what it is that you want God to do. It's best to just solely put your faith and trust in Him. But no matter how it looks, no matter how it seems, no matter how difficult it is, no matter how uncomfortable it is, you must keep your hand in God's hand. If you want Him to bless you, then you must consistently put your faith in Him.

Stop vacillating and wavering in your faith. God is ready to do a new thing in you, but you have to be standing firm. You have to be willing to open up your heart, mind, soul, and spirit to keep your faith in Him.

Your time has come. What God has for you, is for you. Activate your "now faith" and get it! God is just waiting, just waiting to see if this time you'll go all the way for Him. He knows and you know that He's willing and He's able to give you what you need. Know it without a doubt! Activate your now faith and stand firm on this foundational truth.

Reflections in Action

✦ Recognize the times when you tend to waver in your faith, and consciously activate your "now faith" during those situations.

✦ Acknowledge, with conviction, the importance and necessity of faith on your Christian journey.

✦ Keep before you that "faith is the substance of things hoped for."

✦ Trust is a key factor of faith. Once you learn to sincerely trust God, your faith will begin to grow stronger.

✦ Use your faith to encourage yourself when your situation looks bleak.

✦ Take the initiative to activate your faith in difficult times. You must know how to tap into your faith reserve.

✦ When you feel your faith starting to waver, just remember those times that God broke through for you, and know that if He did it then, He will do it again.

✦ Faith will give you the endurance to continue on the journey despite what may be occurring in your life.

✦ Faith will give you a renewed sense of confidence.

✦ Faith is an active process that exists for your now situation— I need a miracle now, I need some help now, I need a cure now. Activate your faith to get what you need now.

✦ Faith opens the door for God to move in your situation, so keep your doors open.

Reflective Prayer

Father God,

In the name of Jesus, I come before you with concerns in my life that look so insurmountable in the natural, that they are making me feel weak in my faith.

I come before you, recognizing that my knees are buckling in the faith, and believing that you will stop the buckling and allow me to stand strong by faith. I need to be strengthened in my faith.

Lord, I need your blessed assurance that even though my situation has not changed yet, I know in faith that you have the final word.

God, encourage me and give me a "now faith." Lord, I need the faith fortitude that only you can give. God, please give me an undeniable, unshakable faith in you, so much so that I will be convicted and convinced that you can and you will do what you promised me in the faith. I know that you can do anything, but fail.

Today my faith and my will are lined up with your desire, your power, and your will. I believe in you and I trust you in all things.

God, thank you for creating a faith place in me that depends and relies on you.

I love you and I thank you that my faith says yes to your will and way for my life. In Jesus' name I pray.

Amen.

5

Stay Focused

Just then a woman who had been subject to bleeding for twelve years came up behind him and touched the edge of his cloak. She said to herself, "If I only touch his cloak, I will be healed." Jesus turned and saw her. "Take heart, daughter," he said, "your faith has healed you." And the woman was healed from that moment.

(MATTHEW 9:20-22)

And a woman having an issue of blood twelve years, which had spent all her living upon physicians, neither could be healed of any, came behind him, and touched the border of his garment: and immediately her issue of blood stanched. And Jesus said, "Who touched me?" When all denied, Peter and they that were with him said, "Master, the multitude throng thee and press thee, and sayest thou, Who touched me?" And Jesus said, "Somebody hath touched me: for I perceive that virtue is gone out of me." And when the woman saw that she was not hid, she came trembling, and falling down before him, she declared unto him before all the people for what cause she had touched him, and how she was healed immediately. And he said unto her, "Daughter, be of good comfort: thy faith hath made thee whole; go in peace."

(LUKE 8:43-48 KJV)

*M*y sisters, this woman with the 12-year issue of blood provides a clear example of what it means to *stay focused*. She knew what she had to do to receive her healing. She stayed focused and she succeeded in touching the hem of Jesus' garment. Despite the pain and embarrassment that her condition surely must have caused her, despite how people must have talked about her, despite how people shunned her, despite all of that, she pressed her way to Jesus where she knew she would receive her healing.

The lesson is clear for the women of God: When you're looking for God to work a miracle in your life, you have got to stay focused on Him. It's so easy to get distracted and to start seeking a quick fix to solve your problems. But as our sister with the issue of blood clearly demonstrates, you must have the internal fortitude to wait on the Lord and stay focused.

What are you waiting for God to do for you? What is blocking you from being all that God desires you to be? While you are waiting for God to move in your life, you must be sure that your actions are in accordance with the will of God. When we try to do things our way and try to remedy things with the power of our own will, we find ourselves distracted and stymied. When we try to impose our will in any given situation, we take our focus off God.

We need to face the reality that there are some things holding us back that only the Lord can root out. Instead of seeking God's healing power, we choose to wallow in our mess. Instead of opening ourselves up before the Lord, we choose to camouflage our issues. We walk around and act like we've got it all together.

It is essential that we ask God to check us out every once in a while. Our journey of faith is an interactive one. You have got to ask in order to receive. We are constantly being refined in faith and spirit. But this refinement does not happen automatically. You have to actively seek God and consciously reveal yourself to Him.

In Second Corinthians 5:17 (KJV), Paul writes, "if any man [or woman] be in Christ, he is a new creature, old things are passed away, behold all things are become new." The act of renewal is an ongoing process. It involves letting go of those things that grieve the very heart of God. It means releasing those things that we know we should no longer be a part of. After you let go of the things that have been hindering your spiritual growth, you must move towards God. You must shift your focus from the temporal to the eternal.

I don't want you to read this and think that your change will happen in an instant. In some cases, it might. But you have got to have the faith reserve to stay focused while you wait on the Lord. I know that it can be difficult to remain committed and stay focused when your issues are nagging at your soul. Unresolved issues can steal our joy and sap our energy. Unresolved issues make us uneasy. When we feel that we are seeking resolutions in faith, and the issues remain unresolved we often find ourselves disappointed, depressed, discouraged, distraught, and disgusted. But it is usually when we discover that our issues won't let us go, no matter what we do, that we find ourselves in a place where we need God to break through and set us free. The moment we declare that we don't want our unresolved issues to obstruct our consistent service to God, He will begin a work in us.

The scriptures show us a woman with a consistent irritation, an annoyance, an unresolved problem, and a serious need for a solution. When you have an issue that has not changed over time, if it is serious enough, it can become life threatening. It can suffocate you. It can stop you in your tracks. It can exhaust you, and it can wipe you out. The woman with the issue of blood had clearly had enough. For 12 long years she had lived with an unresolved issue. The historical and hermeneutical contexts reveal that Levitical law required that if a woman had an issue with blood for many days, then she was considered unclean. Let me break that down. This sister was separated from people for 4,380 days because she was considered unclean. Her life was literally flowing out of her. She was a social outcast; she was rejected. No one hugged her or touched her once during her 12-year ordeal.

This sister needed a solution. In Luke 8:43, the Bible says the woman spent, not some, but all of her living on physicians, and none of them could heal her. During that time doctors often prescribed onions and wine and other noxious mixtures to cure women with blood issues. Over the years, I would imagine that she did and tried everything to try and save her own life. For 12 years she was dying, day by day and drop by drop.

Then she heard about Jesus healing the sick and providing deliverance for the oppressed. She was probably beyond ecstatic when she learned that Jesus had returned to the area. As Jesus approached, she probably sat somewhere in an unassuming place and in an unnoticeable posture. But she was intelligently, strategically, and intentionally planning a way to get to Jesus.

She was focused. In her wretched, rejected, broken, lonely, weak, weary, worn out state of disparity—she stayed focused. As she made her way to Jesus, she believed that God would heal her. Her faith had overcome her hopelessness. As the Bible says, "Faith is the substance of things hoped for, the evidence of things not seen."

Matthew records what this sister had purposed in her mind: "If I may touch his garment, I shall be whole." She knew that if she could get to Jesus, she would be healed. She knew that if she could just make contact, she would be whole again. The same is true for us. If we can conjure up enough energy to touch the hem of His garment, we will live. If we can touch Heaven, Heaven will touch us back. If we remain focused, if we don't back up from the things of God, if we just praise Him and worship Him, anyhow, we will make it. We will survive. If we just stay focused, we will live.

Although hope caused the woman with the issue of blood to seek Jesus, it was her faith that thrust her, energized her, pushed her, and drove her to touch Him.

As the theologian Paul Tillich states in his book *Dynamics of Faith*, this woman probably experienced the birth of a "faith consciousness" in the midst of her issue that embraced her total personality. This steadfast faith transcends every surrounding interference. This great faith moves beyond issues, circumstances, and situations. This unshakable faith moves beyond human weaknesses, beyond loneliness, rejection, and brokenness. This rooted faith moves beyond racism, classism, and sexism. This sustaining faith moves you beyond feeling broke, busted, and disgusted. This unmovable faith overcomes your big hips, big bust size, and big shoe size. This faith allows you to take charge of your situation. Stay focused.

Tillich further states that when you activate this faith, it eradicates the thought patterns that stagnate you. Faith moves you beyond the natural realm into the supernatural realm. Faith is the driving force that enables you to stay focused and determined to get what you need from God. Stay focused.

My sisters, in order to reach this level of faith, like the woman with the issue of blood, we must stay focused. We must press our way to Jesus, like she did, on her hands and knees, bleeding, crawling, and weaving between legs and feet with dirt and dust on her face. We must yearn to touch Jesus like she did. We should get excited by the opportunity to simply glimpse Jesus' robe. We must feel the quickening in her spirit that she felt when she saw the tassel, on a robe worn only by a Rabbi, blowing in the wind.

Matthew writes that the moment she touched Jesus' garment, her hemorrhaging immediately dried up and that Jesus said to her, "your faith has healed you." Luke writes that her issue "stanched," and the blood stopped immediately and that Jesus said, "thy faith has made thee whole." I cannot write it any plainer for you, my sisters. It's as simple as this—Jesus heals.

When Jesus heals you, there is evidence of His healing. When Jesus eliminates your issues, there is evidence that they are gone. When Jesus saves your soul and makes you whole, the change in you will be evident.

The sister with the issue of blood makes it very clear for you and for me that our ability to stay focused is tied to our healing. This sister with the issue of blood was focused. She was determined to put all of her faith and trust in Jesus Christ to get her healing. We too, must put our faith and trust in God through Jesus Christ. If we do, He has promised that He will heal us and give us Holy Ghost Power.

Sisters, it's time to put an end to your slow death. Stop allowing life to drain you day by day and drop by drop. Don't you let any issue in your life stop you from becoming what God desires you to be. Dare to reach out and touch the hem of His garment and be healed. Stay focused. Go in faith; go in peace; go in joy; go with victory; go with your anointing; go with your purpose; go with significance; go with understanding; go with determination; go forth toward your destiny. Don't let anything deter you. Be committed! Be determined! Be unstoppable! Stay focused! Stay focused! Stay focused!

Reflections in Action

- ✦ Remember God wants us to stay focused on the journey.

- ✦ Proclaim the greatness of Christ who is within you when you feel weak and unfocused.

- ✦ Ponder daily the things that you need God to perform in your life.

- ✦ Resist the temptation to fix things on your own: Give it to God.

- ✦ Refuse to allow the world to interfere with your ability to stay focused.

- ✦ Recognize those things that distract you and prevent you from remaining focused.

- ✦ Remember that the longer you are waiting for God, the harder it will be for you to stay focused.

- ✦ Seek direction from the Lord when you are trying to identify what actions you need to take in a given situation.

- ✦ Dedicate daily prayer time to help you remain focused on God in the midst of trouble.

- ✦ Remain determined and on track, focused and faithful, and anticipate and expect that God will bring His promises to pass in your life.

Reflective Prayer

Father God,

I come recognizing that there are times when I have trouble staying focused. I recognize that there are times when I am easily distracted.

There are even times when I have strayed away from you, and I know that I should have stayed on track.

I realize that in the faith, I must remain steadfast and focused because the enemy wants me to be distracted by my problems, so that I will be disappointed in you. For when I am distracted and disappointed, I become distraught and disconnected. When I reach this state, I know I am vulnerable to an attack from the enemy because my faith has been weakened.

Lord, I have decided to get back on track today. I will keep my heart, my mind, and my soul focused on you.

You alone are the only one, true, and living God. You are all powerful and I know that you can do everything that I need you to do in my life.

No matter what happens, I will hold on to my faith in you. I am focused on who you are and who I am to you. You are my loving Father, and I am your blessed daughter.

Thank you for loving me. In Jesus' name I pray.

Amen.

PART TWO

Our Sisters ❧

6

Joy! I Want it Back

And the angel came in unto her, and said, "Hail, thou that art highly favoured, the Lord is with thee: blessed art thou among women." And when she saw him, she was troubled at his saying, and cast in her mind what manner of salutation this should be. And the angel said unto her, "Fear not, Mary: for thou hast found favour with God. And, behold, thou shalt conceive in thy womb, and bring forth a son, and shalt call his name Jesus."

(Luke 1:28-31 KJV)

My sisters, it is time for us to stand steadfast and unmovable and confront that thing which has stolen our joy. I want it back; my joy, I want it back. It might be a situation on your job, or a troubled relationship, or a failing marriage, or an unresolved issue with a family member. Whatever that issue is that has you bound and has stolen your joy, it's time to get your joy back.

To get your joy back, you've got to be willing to recognize that thing that has stolen it in the first place. What is it that steals your joy? What brings tears to your eyes? What is unresolved? What do you need God to do for you? What has God spoken to you and promised to you? What has weighed you down and worn you out?

You know what it is, because whenever it even crosses your mind, it brings you down, it brings tears to your eyes, and it decreases your faith reserve. It blocks you from getting closer to God. For some of us, this thing that has stolen our joy did not happen overnight. No, the enemy has been stealing our joy piece by piece for years. Satan has taken something special from us, and its absence saddens us, and it shakes our faith foundation. When we confront our situations, we are actively taking our circumstances and bringing them before God. Give your situation to the Lord, and trust and believe that He will do what He said.

We've prayed and we've cried about it. But God says, "Enough is enough!" It's time we got our joy back. The good news is that God can restore your joy right now as you read, reflect, and meditate.

God wants us to understand that regardless of what has us bound, and no matter what our circumstances may be, we have to decide that we want the spirit of joy to be restored. The joy of the Lord is your strength. Therefore, sisters, we must truly believe that weeping may endure for a night, but joy really does come in the morning. In other words, this thing that has stolen your joy has got to pass. I, too, have had to go through some things in my life that threatened to wipe me out and steal my joy.

My mother has been fighting lymphoma for years. In addition, my stepfather, Daddy Leonard, is going through dialysis. A few years ago, my one and only younger brother, who is now 50 years old, was playing basketball. He went up for a lay-up, fell, and lost consciousness. It turned out that his fourth and fifth vertebras are fused together. It was a birth defect that no one ever knew he had. He could have been a quadriplegic, but God kept him all these years. To this day, he has never needed surgery to correct this defect, and he is still quite physically active. It's a difficult thing to experience your loved ones dealing with health challenges. Yet, through all of that, I refused to let the enemy steal my joy.

In fact, I told the enemy then, and I've been telling him ever since, "You should have wiped me out when I was born." I weighed a little over two pounds at birth. The doctors declared that I would not live. But God spared my life. The enemy should've taken me out then, when I was in that incubator. His plan was for me to have died

56 years ago. I told the enemy recently, and I'm telling him right now, "You will not steal my joy." My sisters, the time will come on this journey of faith when you will have to boldly proclaim, "You will not wipe me out. You cannot have my joy."

Mary, the Mother of Jesus, has given us the supreme example of how to fight for our joy. Mary was a poor peasant girl who was engaged to Joseph. She was a young woman living her life in Nazareth, when Gabriel visited her. The angel Gabriel greets Mary and informs her that she is highly favored. Then Gabriel tells Mary that the Lord is with her, and she is blessed among women. Mary was troubled by this, and she wondered how what Gabriel said could be true. Mary initially did not understand what Gabriel was saying to her. Her circumstances and her surroundings would not allow her to embrace what she was being told in the Lord: first, that she was highly favored; second, that the Lord was with her; and third, that she was blessed among women.

Mary had been looked upon and treated like property, and yet God identified her and spoke his blessings upon her life. My sisters, Mary, like many women today, didn't see herself the way God saw her. When we don't embrace our self-worth, we get blinded by our struggles. We miss the fact that we are favored by God.

Some people think that they are the only ones favored because they've attained certain positions in life. When they enter a room, they walk in and look around to see if everybody is looking at them. "Don't you see me? I am highly favored. I am the anointed one." No matter where you come from, be it the ghetto or the pinnacle of high society, we were all created in God's image. Sisters, embrace the fact that God's favor is upon you, though not in a manner that puts others down, but in a manner that exalts the presence of God within you.

In Luke 1:30, Gabriel says "Fear not, Mary: for thou hast found favour with God." Maybe you need to get delivered from fear to get your joy back. Fear can bind you. Fear can lock up your emotions. Fear can hold you hostage and stop you from moving forward and prevent you from stepping into your purpose. When you are living in your purpose, you'll have unspeakable joy. When you're living outside of your purpose, you may find that you experience unhappiness, depression, and unrest.

Gabriel, in Luke 1:30, reiterates to Mary that she has found favor with God. I want to suggest that Mary's favor was connected with how she lived her life. God was pleased with her. I'm sure you've heard that favor is not fair, and I believe it to be true. I believe there is a spiritual connection between how we live our lives in the sight of God and how we receive God's favor.

There are levels of favor. Mary wasn't just favored, she was "highly favored." When we are living in God's favor, God must be glorified. The favor is not upon you for *you* to be exalted. The favor is upon you so that God will get the glory. When God is not being glorified in the life of she who is favored, usually the favor starts to fade. The anointing may or may not stay, the gifts may or may not operate, and the favor fades bit by bit when God is not being glorified in our lives.

Gabriel continues to tell Mary what God is going to do in her life:

✦ she will conceive and bring forth a son
✦ she shall call His name Jesus
✦ He shall be great
✦ He shall be called the Son of the Highest
✦ He shall be given the throne of His father, David
✦ He shall reign over the house of Jacob forever
✦ there shall be no end to His kingdom

In considering all that Gabriel has told her, Mary questioned how this should come to pass because she was a virgin. Mary's purity of body and soul sets her up to receive God's favor.

Gabriel answers her question and says:

✦ the holy ghost shall come upon thee
✦ the power of the highest shall overshadow thee
✦ the holy thing shall be called the Son of God

Mary found favor in God's sight because she had been purified and refined from all corruption by the overshadowing of the Holy Ghost. Gabriel confirms this supernatural event by informing Mary that her cousin, Elisabeth, who was barren and well beyond child-bearing years, was six months pregnant. At this news, Mary's fear instantly turns into faith. Her doubts and her concerns turn into confidence. And Mary, this poor peasant girl, this young virgin who had been viewed as property, this young unwed mother who was engaged to Joseph, now speaks with clarity, with confidence, and with boldness, "Behold the handmaid of the Lord; be it unto me according to thy word" (Luke 1:38). And with those words, Mary surrenders totally to the will of God.

My sisters, you must embrace what the Lord has spoken to you, and you must totally surrender to the will of God, so that you can get your joy back. Some of you profess to be saved, sanctified, and filled with the Holy Ghost, and yet you're suffering from deep bouts of depression. You aren't showing your so-called joy of Jesus to anybody. You've got an attitude 24/7.

If God has spoken a word to you, then it is time that you proclaim it, repeat it, and rest in it. God is calling us to a place of surrender. Don't allow anything to steal your joy while you're going through and waiting on God.

The Bible records in Luke 1:39-41, that Mary went to Elisabeth's house. When Elisabeth heard Mary's voice, her baby leapt for joy in the womb, and Elisabeth was filled with the Holy Ghost. My sisters, here is where the real lesson is for us as women. In Luke 1:42-44, Elisabeth confirms what God has spoken when she tells her cousin Mary that she is blessed among women and blessed is the fruit of her womb. In speaking those words, Elisabeth encourages and reaffirms Mary.

Women of God, we must encourage each other. There is a dire need for women to affirm other women. It pains my spirit when I see women shunning other women. You work with other women every day, yet you walk right by them and you don't speak to them. You relinquish the opportunity to build up another woman with a simple compliment. You hold back a hello that just might heal her heart.

As Christian women, it is our charge to be open, loving, and willing to encourage another sister. And here's the tricky part, when you encourage another sister, don't expect her to reciprocate. You just do the right thing. Stop hating on your sister and encourage her instead.

I'm very clear about the gifts that God has given me. My grandmother, Mary Koontz, was a sharp, short woman from Bryan, Texas. She was a really strong woman whose demeanor harkened back to Mother Africa. She had the gifts of discernment, wisdom, and knowledge. She had a number of daughters. One of them was my mother, Ruth. And she, too, had the gifts of discernment, wisdom, and knowledge. That gift was also given to me. My grandmother's gifts were sharp, my mother's gifts were sharper, and mine are the sharpest. And Candace, my baby? Her gifts are even sharper than all of ours (and Lord have mercy on my granddaughter, Kaylah Jo Ann, whose gifts, I'm sure, will be phenomenal).

I've learned to use my gifts wisely. I do not allow the enemy to speak mess to me concerning another sister. You cannot allow it either, no matter how intuitive you may be, no matter how well you can read someone else, because a part of having joy on the journey is through the encouragement and the expression of kindness to another sister. When you bless another sister, you feel good and you feel joy on the inside. There's a connection.

Luke 1:45 reads, "And blessed is she that believed: for there shall be a performance of those things which were told her from the Lord." God wants you to know that the promise He made to you shall come to pass. The thing that you've been waiting for shall be. That thing that brought sadness to your heart shall be no more. You will not shed any more tears about it, and you shall no longer suffer depression as a result of it. Your joy is about to be restored.

The same supernatural power that overshadowed Mary is the same power that shall overshadow you. The Bible declares in Luke 1:46-47, that Mary said, "My soul doth magnify the Lord, and my spirit hath rejoiced in God my Saviour." Mary recognized the reality of God's might and His mercy. He was about to turn the existing order upside down through the child in her womb. Mary's joy overcame her because the promise that God made at the beginning of time was going to be fulfilled through her womb. A peasant girl in the city of Nazareth was about to become the mother of the Savior of the world.

Just like Mary, we need to know that God will come through for us. We need to know, like Mary knew, that what God has promised, He will bring to pass. He can and He will work miracles on our behalf, if we don't get weighed down, and if we don't get heavy in our souls. Remember the joy you used to have? It can be yours again. The world didn't give it to you and the world can't take it away. Joy, I want it back.

The power to reclaim your joy resides in your praise. Oh, magnify the Lord with me and rejoice in God our Savior. You shall be full of joy again. Make a joyful noise unto the Lord. Count it all joy. What you have sowed in tears, you shall reap in joy. Weeping, crying, and the gnashing of teeth may endure for a night, but joy shall come in the morning.

Joy, I want it back. I want it back! I want it back! Sisters, we must refuse to spend another day with our heads hanging down with the weight of the world on our shoulders. We must refuse to walk around looking pitiful and sad. This is not the time to give in to fatigue and defeat. We must praise God anyhow. No matter what we might find ourselves confronted with, we have no choice but to praise God anyhow. When the praises go up, the joy will come down. The joy of the Lord is our strength. Your joy is wrapped up in your praise. You can't praise God and be mad at the same time. You can't praise God and be depressed at the same time. If you're depressed and you start praising, you will get happy. There is a connection between our praise and our joy.

It's time we got our lives together and our thoughts together. It's time we decided to stay away from that other woman's husband. It's time we stopped dressing provocatively at work. It's time for us to move into a new place in the Lord. It's a new day. If you want God to fulfill His promises to you, then you must get yourself lined up with God's will. Stop doing those things that are displeasing in His sight. Sisters, it's time for us to get ourselves together and get our joy back!

How can we glorify God, if we walk around looking like we're sucking on lemons or drinking vinegar because things are not going the way we planned? Don't you get it? God has the power to do exceedingly abundantly above all we could think or imagine. So what if your husband or your boyfriend left you? God has got a better man for you. So what if you're still single or divorced? If God said He will give you the desires of your heart, He will. So live your life accordingly. God can give you the thing you desire the most when you least expect it. If it is ordained for you, it's for you. No demon in hell can stop what God has ordained for you. Think "reciprocity." Your joy is directly associated with how you live your life. There's a connection. Joy, I want it back.

Now let's get our joy back. To get it back, we must pray. But not only for the reinstatement of our own joy: I want you to pray for the return of your sister's joy. I want you to pray that we will all begin the process of knowing, of being commissioned, of being taught, of being encouraged. I want us to embrace the opportunity to encourage another sister. Find a sister to be your prayer partner, and together pray for the collective reinstatement of our joy. Joy, we want it back!

Reflections in Action

+ Hold on to your joy regardless of your circumstances.

+ Take authority over the enemy.

+ Know that you are favored and graciously accept it.

+ See yourself as God sees you, as a queen with godly humility. Don't walk around as if you are better than everybody else.

+ Know that God is always with you and that you are blessed.

+ Stand against fear.

+ Glorify God at all times.

+ Tell yourself aloud, "I want my joy back." Reclaim it, repeat it, and rest in God's word to you.

+ Don't let anyone or anything steal your joy.

+ Bless, encourage, and affirm another sister.

+ Let the Lord strengthen your faith.

+ Purpose in your heart to praise God anyhow.

Reflective Prayer

Father God,

I have a heaviness in my heart and I have lost my joy. Life has weighed me down and I recognize that the enemy has cunningly stepped into the back door of my life and has stolen my joy.

Right now, I declare that the enemy must return my joy in Jesus' name.

The minute that declaration left my lips, I know it was done. I know that my joy shall be restored because I know that there is nothing too hard for you.

I believe in my heart that the promises that you made to me will come to pass and you will do just what you said you would do for me. So in the meantime, I won't walk around feeling sad and looking defeated. Instead, I will worship you and praise you in advance of the blessings.

While I am waiting, I will be continually calling on your name. I know you will restore my joy. I can already see myself in the supernatural—clapping my hands, stomping my feet, and I can clearly hear the joy bells ringing in my soul.

I speak your joy back into my life and I thank you now for my joy. I got it back! In Jesus' name I pray.

Amen.

7

The Victim, the View, and the Victory

But Jesus went to the Mount of Olives. At dawn he appeared again in the temple courts, where all the people gathered around him, and he sat down to teach them. The teachers of the law and the Pharisees brought in a woman caught in adultery. They made her stand before the group and said to Jesus, "Teacher, this woman was caught in the act of adultery. In the Law Moses commanded us to stone such women. Now what do you say?" They were using this question as a trap, in order to have a basis for accusing him. But Jesus bent down and started to write on the ground with his finger. When they kept on questioning him, he straightened up and said to them, "If any one of you is without sin, let him be the first to throw a stone at her." Again he stooped down and wrote on the ground. At this, those who heard began to go away one at a time, the older ones first, until only Jesus was left, with the woman still standing there. Jesus straightened up and asked her, "Woman, where are they? Has no one condemned you?" "No one, sir," she said. "Then neither do I condemn you," Jesus declared. "Go now and leave your life of sin."

(JOHN 8:1-11)

My sisters, how much does what other people say about you affect you? Do you fall victim to other people's perceptions of you? How is being a victim impeding your spiritual growth? Do you believe that you have what it takes to fulfill the destiny that

God has for you? Do you realize that when you allow yourself to live as a victim, you are living beneath your potential to live a victorious life?

The sister in John 8:1-11 was living a victimized life. She was accused of committing one of the worst sins of her time. She was an adulteress. But the truth of the matter is that she wasn't only a perpetrator, she was also a victim. She was a victim of her times. During Biblical times, women were considered property and were often used to produce sons. Because she was considered property and therefore was at the disposal of men, we have to question whether she actually consented to participate in this adulterous act. We have to question it because we don't have the background information. Women were victimized because they rarely had opportunity to have any input concerning their lives. When you find yourself in a situation where you have no advocate to speak on your behalf and no one to stand up for your rights, after awhile, you begin to assume a victimized spirit. You start walking like a victim, you start talking like a victim, you start acting like a victim, you start reacting and responding like a victim, and you are unable to view yourself beyond how others view you. You begin to acquiesce and tolerate various forms of abuse and mistreatment. You begin to live beneath your birthright as a daughter of the Most High God. You fall into the trap of living as a victim as opposed to living as a victor because of someone else's view of you and your distorted view of yourself.

As women, we live in a society that is constantly trying to deny us access to our rightful places in the kingdom of God. In fact, we often deny these rights ourselves because when we view ourselves as victims, we can't stand to see anybody else live victoriously. Some of us have risen to places in corporate America, in government, in the church, and in academia where we can reach back and pull another sister up, but we do not, because we've allowed ourselves to be victimized along the way. Once we make it, we start telling ourselves, "I made my own way to the top. Nobody helped me, so therefore I will not help her." It's a shame when we reach that pinnacle of success only to have forgotten where we came from and how we got to the top. Once we think we've made it, our view of others and our view of ourselves tend to change (and not always for the best).

Consider this real-life example. Anybody who knows me knows that if you approach me and address me as "Sister Browning," I will correct you. I'll say, "Call me Pastor Jo Ann or Reverend Browning, please." I do that because your refusal to use my proper title dishonors God and dishonors the pastoral office that God has appointed me to assume. It's nothing personal, but I cannot let your view of me interfere with God's calling on my life. I cannot allow your view of me to victimize me. It's hard enough for women in the pulpit as it is. It's a fact; I can't ever remember a time, when we were both standing together, that anyone ever called my husband, the Senior Pastor of Ebenezer A.M.E. Church, Brother Browning. He is always referred to as Pastor Browning or Reverend Browning.

If you view yourself as others view you, and you begin to embrace a victimized spirit, you will miss your place in the kingdom of God. If you can't see yourself as God sees you because you have a victimized spirit, then your view will be out of whack. If you view yourself as less than how God sees you, then you will not be able to see yourself in the place that God has for you.

John 8:1-11 provides a perfect example of how your view can lead to your victimization and cost you your victory. But first, we must consider what happens in John 7:14. Jesus returns to the temple, after having taught there the day before. Jesus knew that the Jews were seeking to kill Him. Why did they want to kill Him? They wanted to kill Him because they viewed Him as a threat.

I want you to understand who was present when Jesus returned to the temple. Jesus was teaching the scribes. They were laymen who cared for the temple and the archives of sacred literature. They were not priests, but they worked with the priests. The scribes and the priests were against Jesus. The Pharisees were also there. These men were separatists. They were strict observers of the law and they had great political power. They felt that they were chosen to preserve, interpret, and teach the Jewish law.

The scribes and Pharisees brought a woman before Jesus. She was a nameless woman. The Bible does not tell us anything specific about her. All we know is that she was a woman who had been arrested because she committed adultery. The Bible is clear in its condemnation of adultery. In fact, it is referenced in three separate instances:

1. Exodus 20:14: "You shall not commit adultery."
2. Deuteronomy 5:18: "You shall not commit adultery."
3. Deuteronomy 22:22: "If a man is found sleeping with another man's wife, both the man who slept with her and the woman must die. You must purge the evil from Israel."

I question the validity of the charges leveled against this sister. Remember, she was considered property. She had no rights. That means she had no choice in this so-called adulterous act. Furthermore, adultery is a consensual sexual intercourse between two parties. The Bible says both parties must be condemned. So, where was her co-conspirator? Why wasn't he brought into the full view of the crowd?

The leaders brought her into a temple full of people. They wanted everyone present to view her. But where was the man? It takes two to commit the act of adultery, yet they brought only the woman into view. The scribes and the Pharisees victimized her. They labeled her as an adulteress all by herself. The crowd immediately viewed her as a worthless sinner.

This sister had been caught in the act. Imagine her standing there in the full view of the crowd. She was probably only partially clothed, if at all. Her lover must have stayed behind to get himself together, while she was pulled through the streets, all the way to the temple, to stand in the midst of everybody. She was viewed as a sinner. She was a victim, and nothing about this situation looked as if it would lead to a victory for her.

To those who viewed her, the arrest was undoubtedly justified because she was caught in the act. She was an adulteress. But she was also a victim, because her lover was not arrested. Think about it. If she was arrested in the act, he had to be there. He **had** to be there. He **had** to be there. The scribes and the Pharisees couldn't have missed him.

If she was arrested in the act, he had to be there. You cannot commit adultery by yourself. She was a victim in her wrongdoing. I don't condone what she did, but she should not have had to suffer their condemnation all by herself on display for all to see. Based on my theological education, my research, and my knowledge of the

Jewish culture, it was pure bias and sexism that exposed her and shielded her lover.

As she stood before the crowd, in full view, barely clothed, exposed, the Pharisees begin to quote the law and demand that she be stoned. But they tried to trick Jesus when they asked Him, "In the Law, Moses commanded us to stone such women. Now what do you say?" In other words, what do you say about this, Jesus? What do you say about her? They posed a trick question. But Jesus knew the law just like the Pharisees. Jesus knew it was a setup. They wanted Jesus to disagree with the law so that they could arrest Him.

My sisters, Jesus was viewed as a threat. He was also a victim because the scribes and Pharisees wanted to destroy Him. Jesus understood the woman. Jesus knew who He was and what He could do for her. Jesus was and He still is victorious in all things. He has the power to give that victory to us, and He is so willing to give it. The Bible says that Jesus stooped down without hesitation and wrote on the ground with His finger as though He heard them not. In other words, Jesus ignored them.

You might ask, if Jesus ignored them, who was He listening to? Perhaps, He was listening to His Father. He had shut them out and tuned in to God the Father. He listened to His daddy. When He stooped down He humbled himself. Here was this adulteress standing before Him, and Jesus the Christ stoops down and humbles himself.

My sisters, every time Jesus healed someone He would look at them or He would look up, but He never stooped down. He used His body language to speak to the woman when He stooped down and began to write. He said something to the Pharisees and the Sadducees. The woman knew she was an adulteress. Yet Jesus did not belittle her. People will belittle you. When they view you in a low moment, they will try to make you feel like you're dirt. Jesus is compassionate.

Victory comes in the way you handle yourself when you've been victimized. If you are a woman and you haven't been victimized yet, you will be. How you respond will dictate whether you will live a defeated life or a victorious one. How you respond will dictate whether God gets the glory or not. How you respond will dictate your ability to rise above the victimization.

The scribes and the Pharisees continued to press Jesus for an answer. As Jesus lifted himself up, I know He blew their minds when He said, "If any one of you is without sin, let him be the first to throw a stone at her."

It's clear that Jesus read the hearts and the minds of the people. It's clear that He knew each one of their sins. They had accused and condemned this woman. It was easy for them to justify because her sin was out there in plain view. But Jesus viewed her as a child of God. He knew that everyone who saw her as a sinner was also a sinner. My sisters, you have to be careful where you point your finger, because the truth is that everybody has some stuff in her closet. If you're prepared to throw stones at another sister, you'd better make sure you have found a place to hide from the stones that will be thrown back at you. Through Jesus' love, compassion, sensitivity, and forgiveness, our adulterous sister found her victory.

The Bible says Jesus stooped down again and wrote on the ground. As He wrote, each of the scribes and Pharisees who had been so ready to hurl stones at the accused was being convicted by his own conscience and they began to leave one by one. The Bible says that from the oldest to the youngest, the hypocrisy of all who accused had now been exposed. When you have Jesus in your life, He will protect you from your enemies, even if the odds are stacked up against you and it seems impossible for you to live a victorious life.

After they all left, and Jesus was left alone with the woman, He stood up and He spoke to her directly. When Jesus is in control of your life, He will speak directly to you. He asked her, "Woman, where are they? Has no one condemned you?" The King James Version of the scripture says she replied, "No man, Lord." She acknowledged Him as Lord. The scribes and Pharisees didn't acknowledge Him as Lord. They called Jesus "master" and "teacher," but she acknowledged Him as her Savior.

My sisters, Jesus wants to be our Lord, our Savior, and our protector. Why do we continue to wail in self-pity and wallow in life's issues and problems, when Jesus is standing right beside us? We do not have to play the victim. Jesus wants us to have the victory. God wants us to yield to Him and change our viewpoint so that we see ourselves the way He sees us. The enemy wants to keep us bound by what other people think and what other people see. The enemy wants to skew our view and make us think we cannot be free from all our sins. But God is able to cast off our enemies and make them our footstools. God holds our victory in the very palms of His hands.

My sisters, it is time that you view yourself the way God views you. God has great things in store for His daughters. If you pay attention, you will see that God is positioning women to be the head and not the tail in all areas of His kingdom. It was an incredible moment in time when Reverend Vashti McKenzie was elected as the first female bishop of the African Methodist Episcopal church after 213 years. The church didn't view women as bishops. Many thought it was too soon for a woman to be a bishop. It had already been 213 years—too soon?

Bishop McKenzie did not let anyone else's viewpoints dictate her destiny. The world may not have viewed her as a bishop, but God did. Bishop McKenzie was able to view herself through God's lens. She did not allow other people's viewpoints to victimize her. She did not fall victim to sexism. She knew she could rest in her anointing and she saw herself as God saw her—as a bishop. God gave her the victory. My sisters, you've got to see it to believe it, and then you must believe it to achieve it.

My sisters, some of us have been walking, talking, acting, and reacting as a victim for so long that we do not know how *not* to be a victim. You have allowed others to view you as you once were, before Jesus saved your soul, but old things have passed away. You are brand new now. Jesus loves us so much. He wants us to live victoriously. Therefore, in spite of other people's views, in spite of being victims of a sometimes sexist society, we have the victory through Jesus Christ.

Jesus is stooping down and writing in the sands of time for you. Your slate has been wiped clean. Your accusers have fled. Their views no longer make a difference. You will no longer be victimized and operate out of a victimized spirit. You have the victory through Jesus Christ. Jesus is speaking directly to us, just as He did to the adulterous woman, "I don't condemn thee." So, go my sisters and sin no more. Go and sin no more. No more, no more.

Reflections in Action

✦ The power of perception resides in how you see yourself. Do not allow other people's perceptions to victimize you.

✦ Be determined to see yourself as God sees you.

✦ Recognize the fact that we are all sinners, but we serve a forgiving God.

✦ Don't let your past keep you from embracing your future.

✦ Victimization is a halting state of mind, but you can be set free in Christ Jesus.

✦ Do not allow your victories to be delayed because you are stuck in the pain of your past.

✦ Always remember that you are a child of the Most High God, and as such, God has already given you the victory.

✦ Look around and embrace your place in the kingdom through the eyes of God and not through the eyes of others.

✦ If you recognize that you have been living your life as a victim because you have allowed other people's viewpoints to define you, decide this moment to stop being a victim, and watch God make you victorious.

Reflective Prayer

Father God,

I thank you that I, who had been viewed as a victim and who had walked around with a victimized spirit, shall now walk in victory. I thank you and praise you for what you are doing in my life today and I know that the best is yet to come.

Father God, in the name of Jesus, I thank you for deliverance. I thank you dear Lord for a clearer view. I thank you dear Heavenly Father that I am no longer a victim. I understand that I am now victorious. I accept the victory. I thank you for what you've done in the lives of so many women.

Thank you Lord for picking me up when I fell down. Thank you Lord for delivering me and setting me free. Thank you Lord for making me a victorious woman.

Now God, bless your women. May we walk in victory from this day forward, and may our enemies stay off our backs and off our trails. We are women, God, who have fallen down, but we've gotten back up again in you. We thank you dear Heavenly Father that we shall not turn back to those things that made us feel like victims. We thank you dear Heavenly Father that we have been wonderfully and marvelously made in your sight. We thank you dear Lord that you do not make mistakes. And for this sweet and comforting knowledge, we praise your name.

Bless us, keep us, guide us, and use us for the building of your kingdom on earth as it is in Heaven. May your grace, love and mercy abound in our lives, and may we always be pleasing in your sight. In Jesus' name we want to say thank you. In Jesus' name we pray.

Amen.

8

The Approach of Abigail
A Woman of Wisdom

One of the servants told Nabal's wife Abigail: "David sent messengers from the desert to give our master his greetings, but he hurled insults at them. Yet these men were very good to us. They did not mistreat us, and the whole time we were out in the fields near them nothing was missing. Night and day they were a wall around us all the time we were herding our sheep near them. Now think it over and see what you can do, because disaster is hanging over our master and his whole household. He is such a wicked man that no one can talk to him."

Abigail lost no time. She took two hundred loaves of bread, two skins of wine, five dressed sheep, five seahs of roasted grain, a hundred cakes of raisins and two hundred cakes of pressed figs, and loaded them on donkeys. Then she told her servants, "Go on ahead; I'll follow you." But she did not tell her husband Nabal.

When Abigail saw David, she quickly got off her donkey and bowed down before David with her face to the ground. She fell at his feet and said: "My lord, let the blame be on me alone. Please let your servant speak to you; hear what your servant has to say. May my lord pay no attention to that wicked man Nabal. He is just like his name—his name is Fool, and folly goes with him. But as for me, your servant, I did not see the men my master sent.

When David heard that Nabal was dead, he said, "Praise be to the LORD, who has upheld my cause against Nabal for treating me with contempt. He has kept his servant from doing wrong and has

*brought Nabal's wrongdoing down on his own head." Then David
sent word to Abigail, asking her to become his wife. His servants
went to Carmel and said to Abigail, "David has sent us to you to
take you to become his wife."*

*She bowed down with her face to the ground and said, "Here is your
maidservant, ready to serve you and wash the feet of my master's
servants." Abigail quickly got on a donkey and, attended by her five
maids, went with David's messengers and became his wife.*

(1 SAMUEL 25:14-19, 23-25, 39-42)

*M*y sisters, are you haunted by something you said or did in
the past? Does a past decision that you made ever keep you
up at night? Do you find yourself facing feelings of regret every time
you think about it? It is time for us to stop regretting the past. It's
time for us to build up our character and learn how to feel comfortable in how we approach life's difficulties. It's time that we learn
how to seek God's wisdom in our decision-making process so that we
no longer respond out of our own will and desire when we must
make life-altering decisions.

It's time that we commit ourselves to seeking the Lord for His
wisdom and His guidance, so that we can make the right choices.
Our sister Abigail, a woman of wisdom, provides an excellent
example of how we should lean not to our own understanding, but
should instead trust God to guide us.

From Abigail, we can learn how to approach difficult situations
and how to respond to them. God can give us the supernatural clarity we need to move through situations and avoid the drama. This is
important, women of God, because we have a tendency towards
drama. You know what I'm talking about—we all play into it at times.

As Christian women, we must begin to see ourselves as God sees
us. Now, if you are a sister who always responds with poise, and your
feathers never get ruffled, then this chapter may not apply to you.
But if you are a woman like most of us, who reverts to your old ways
when you are faced with a crisis—if you cry, curse, argue, or just
scream—then read on.

If you have a temper, or a mean streak, or you are prone to flip off at any old time, this chapter is for you. If you've ever gotten so angry that your face got red, your eyes got red, your lips got tight, or your nose flared, then my sister, I wrote this just for you. If you are a woman who is constantly involved in heated arguments and disagreements, then read on. If you've ever regretted something that you said or did in the heat of the moment, then this chapter is for you. It's time that we invite the Lord to shine down His heavenly searchlight and to reveal our combative character. It's the part of us that wants to be difficult, and knows how and when to push other people's hot buttons. Admit it—sometimes you start an argument for no good reason. Sometimes, you just feel like being combative.

The enemy recognizes that combative spirit in us, and he uses it to seek, kill, and destroy our relationships with others. The enemy loves it when he can get you to curse like a sailor. He loves to watch your temper flare up. He dances with joy when you push your husband and your loved ones away with your anger. But if we are who we say we are, if we are indeed daughters of the Most High God, when the dust settles, we regret our behavior. It's time to turn the tables on the enemy.

God wants to address that place in us that falls prey to circumstances and situations, and causes us to behave irrationally. Because when we are in that place, the enemy has a foothold. When we go to that other side, we have relinquished control.

Now let's look at the scripture and how we can approach situations for ourselves with the spirit of Abigail. Consider that before she married David, Abigail was Nabal's wife. Nabal was a very rich man, but he was also a fool. In fact, his very name means fool. The Scripture says Nabal was surly. Nabal was rude and he had a temper. The Bible implies that he was always a fool. It does not say he was once a kind man who became a fool. There is no indication there was a personality change. Abigail, on the other hand, was described as intelligent and wise and beautiful with good understanding and a beautiful countenance.

We have a husband and wife who are total opposites. In terms of personality, they were at two separate ends of the spectrum. Some of you are in relationships like that right now. You realize the difference between yourself and your spouse or significant other. You realize that there is the possibility that there may be a serious problem in the relationship. How you respond to these differences is an indication of your spiritual maturity.

David sends ten of his men to Nabal to ask for provisions in return for the protection that David had provided to Nabal's men during shearing time. David's men had previously provided unsolicited protection for Nabal's shepherds and herdsmen. Nabal makes David's men wait for an answer. My sisters, beware of the wait. Sometimes the devil will mess with you while you wait. The enemy wants to see how you will react when you are uncertain of the outcome. The devil specializes in pauses, delays, and time lapses. Sometimes we let our guard down while we are waiting, and that is when the enemy strikes. He blindsides us with the unexpected.

On your journey of faith, don't let the enemy cause you to slip while you are waiting for a Word from the Lord. You need to know that a delay does not mean a denial from the Lord.

Now Nabal should have responded favorably to David's request, but instead Nabal responded as the meaning of his name dictated, foolishly. Some of us work for a Nabal. Some of us are involved with a Nabal. And just like David's men, you expect one thing and they respond in a completely opposite and unexpected manner. Nabal's response was rude and unnecessary. My sisters, you need to know that the Nabals in your life are going to be rude and mean-spirited. How you respond may determine whether you will be blessed or cursed.

When David's men told him what happened, David was ready to kill that fool. But in First Samuel 25:14, one of the servants tells Abigail about Nabal's reaction. Now notice how Abigail responds in First Samuel 25:18. She did not waste time. She took 200 loaves of bread, 2 skins of wine, sheep, grain, and figs and loaded it on a donkey. Abigail had a plan. She knew what needed to be done to prevent disaster and she took action.

Abigail was respected, she had a godly reputation, she thought before she acted, and then she acted. God is calling you, women of God, to be like Abigail:

◆ be known for your godly reputation

◆ be respected as a woman of God

◆ be rational and wise in your actions and your responses to life's trials

In First Samuel 25:19, the Bible says Abigail gave instructions to the servants, but she did not tell her husband. The conjunction "but" implies here that she should have told him. But she did what she had to do. She should have asked for permission, but she didn't. Abigail knew what she was dealing with—she knew her husband was a fool. And furthermore, she knew he was wrong in his response to David, and because of his foolishness the entire household was in danger. Abigail knew she had to act. She was resourceful and she knew what she had to do. Abigail was a woman of wisdom. She was confident and she was bold in the Lord. Here's the key: she was willing to take a leap of faith.

When Abigail sees David, she quickly dismounts from her donkey and bows down before David with her face to the ground. She falls at his feet and asks him to blame her. Pay attention my sisters and learn from Abigail's wisdom. Abigail's approach to David was humble and strong at the same time.

Now, let's consider what the Bible says in First Samuel 25: 26-31. Abigail had David's ear and at the appointed time, she speaks up. She speaks, first of all, in faith with authority and confidence. She spoke blessings upon David. Did you notice that in reading the text? We all know about the anointing on David. But Abigail also spoke blessings upon David. Abigail spoke prophetically. I'm sure nobody ever told you that Abigail was a prophetess. All you hear is about Nabal's foolishness, but it was Abigail who made the difference.

She spoke protection over David: she spoke metaphorically when she mentioned the pockets of a sling. After all, we all know that David had killed Goliath with a slingshot and a stone. Abigail spoke peace into the situation. When she finished blessing David, she asked him to remember her when the Lord blesses him.

Abigail, with her wisdom, must have warmed David's heart with her honesty and tact. She respected him as king. She gave David a glimpse of God's plan for him even before it came to pass. The approach of Abigail was godly and wise. She made David realize that what he was about to do was unnecessary. David is so grateful to Abigail that he speaks blessings on her life.

When Abigail gets home, Nabal is having a feast and he's very drunk. So she waits until the next day, when he is sober, to tell him what has transpired. Notice that she doesn't tell him while he's drunk, that's because Abigail was a woman of integrity. Nabal had a heart attack or stroke and died ten days later. When David heard of Nabal's death, he rejoiced over the fact that he had been kept from killing him and Abigail became his wife.

Abigail's countenance made the difference. She spoke peace into the midst of confusion. She was wise enough to take charge and do what was best for everyone involved. My sisters, it's time to change our approach. If you are reading this chapter and you know that your response to life's tight situations is not pleasing in God's sight, it's time to change your approach.

It's time for the women of God to be virtuous. Your "David Blessing" may be held up because God is waiting for you to take an "Abigail Approach" to your most difficult situations. It's time that you change the way you respond to the Nabals in your home and on your job. It's time to get rid of that angry, mean-spirited streak that keeps causing you to flip out and lose your religion in the face of adversity.

Every time you give the enemy the opportunity to control you, you hurt God's heart. God wants to heal and deliver that place in you because you have work to do. But God can't use you if you can't control your reactions to life's trials. God must be glorified in our lives.

Mean-spiritedness is a trick of the enemy. If you're wondering why your marriage is failing or why you can't seem to maintain a meaningful relationship, it may be because you've allowed the enemy to have a foothold in your life. You cannot live a dual existence. You can't conduct yourself one way at church, another way at your job, and another way at home. God is looking for consistency in the women of God. Let God cleanse you so that the enemy will not have a foothold in your life anymore.

Reflections in Action

✦ In every intense situation, remember to stop and seek God before you respond.

✦ If you know that you have negative personality traits, and you recognize the need for them to change, and you ask God to change them for you, He will.

✦ If you find your "old self" emerging in crisis situations, ask God to strengthen your "new self," and you will be able to respond in a positive and "brand new" way.

✦ Be willing to acknowledge that there are areas in your life in which you consistently have trouble remaining steadfast in your Christian walk.

✦ After an altercation, in which you know your response was not Christian, consecrate prayer time and ask God for forgiveness.

✦ Work to consistently get to the place that you pause and pray before you "lay your religion down."

✦ Remember that you are God's agent and dedicate yourself to being one of His best.

✦ Remember that God may use you to prevent a disaster in someone's life, so you need to always be ready and available for His service.

✦ Keep before you the desire to maintain a Godly reputation while you journey through life.

✦ God created women in His own image and has given us Godly influence. Use your God-given influence to be a blessing and to glorify God.

Reflective Prayer

Father God,

Wash away anything in me that is not pleasing in your sight. I want to be a virtuous and wise woman in your sight. Please forgive my past actions, my cursing, my screaming, and the hurtful things I may have said to others.

Lord, speak to my heart, speak to my mind, speak to my soul. Let me respond out of your will, respond out of your ways, respond out of your Word. If it had not been for you on my side, I don't know where I would be.

I've faced the reality that there are some Nabals in my life. But I gripped this reality that greater is He that is in me than he that is in the world.

I also realize that there is a need for me to change my approach and response when I am faced with intense situations. I humbly submit my approach and my attitude to you, and I desire in my heart to change in those places where I need to change.

Thank you for saving my soul and making me whole. I feel alright now. I feel like running on to see what the end is going to be.

Father God, in the name of Jesus, I believe you right now. Now shower down your Holy Ghost anointing on me. I bless your name, I magnify you, and I glorify you. In Jesus' name I thank you for the approach of Abigail. In Jesus' name I pray.

Amen.

9

No More Drama

Therefore, if anyone is in Christ, he is a new creation; the old has gone, the new has come!

(2 CORINTHIANS 5:17)

My sisters, do you know a sister who always seems to have a problem? Have you ever witnessed a sister in the midst of a public meltdown? Do you have any sister-friends that you must mentally prepare yourself to talk to, because you know their latest drama has the potential to bring you down also? Are you, yourself, living a drama-filled life?

It is time for us to yield to God's process of eliminating the drama in our lives. In order for us to be all that God has ordained us to be, we must be "drama-free" so that we can yield to the transforming power of God. Think of this process as you would your annual wellness exam. Except, instead of a physical check-up it's time for your annual spiritual check-up. You need to be willing to let God check you out from head to toe. And when He gives you His assessment of your spiritual health, you must submit to do whatever He wants and needs you to do to transform you into the woman that He ordained you to be.

We all need to go to God and be open to whatever changes need to take place in our lives. The routine of life and our daily experiences sometimes cause us to fall into a spiritual rut. We don't always allow God to enlarge our territories. We are often so busy taking care of others that we put what we need spiritually on the back burner of our lives and we neglect to attend to the needs of our souls. We become complacent, satisfied, indifferent, relaxed, and happy-go-lucky. Some of us have convinced ourselves that we have arrived, when, truth be told, we have not.

I encourage you to open yourselves up to a move of God during this season in your life. Release yourself to receive what God has planned for you. I know it is our nature to take care of everyone else but ourselves. But God is calling us to embrace what He intends for us to have for ourselves. Genesis 1:27-28, states that God created women in His image as He created man, and He wanted to bless us as He blessed man.

In other words, God created you with the intent of blessing you. You were created to be blessed. You were created to be the recipient of blessings beyond measure. Therefore, you need to know that whatever you need from God, whatever you may desire, and whatever you have not yet obtained, is on the way. God created you so that He could bless you.

However, in order for God to release His abundant blessings in your life, a change must take place in you. A transformation must take place in our lives in order for God to take us individually and collectively to another place in Him. The change has to take place so that we can be entrusted with the extraordinary things of God, so God will be glorified in our lives. The enemy cannot stop God's blessings from being manifested in our lives. What God has for you really is for you.

We cannot allow the pressures and the stresses of being who we are as grandmothers, mothers, daughters, wives, sisters, and friends to wear us down to the point that we don't do enough for ourselves. My sisters, we have inherited a warped sense of reality, and we have to learn how to give ourselves permission to do for ourselves and live our lives the way God intended us to live, whole and healthy.

We need a transformation that will allow us to recognize and remove the drama from our lives. We need to make some major changes for ourselves and the young women who are coming after us. We need to do it right now.

To truly be transformed by God, we have to be willing to do what needs to be done and make whatever alterations in our lives that need to be made. We have to alter our lifestyles—either let some things out or take some things in. It doesn't matter where you are on your journey of faith or what you need from God. God is waiting for you to posture yourself and yield to His will through Jesus Christ. God is waiting for you to occupy a faith place in Him. But before you can occupy that space in God, you must commit to live a "drama-free" life.

That's what happened to our sister Mary J. Blige. Her song, *No More Drama,* is all about her decision to rise above the drama in her life: from the father who left her, to the men who broke her heart, to the drugs that almost destroyed her, to the women who hurt her. She was tired of dealing with the drama in her life:

> *To find your happiness*
> *I don't know*
> *Only God knows where the story ends*
> *For me*
> *But I know where the story begins*
> *It's up to us to choose*
> *Whether we win or lose*
> *And I choose to win*

My sisters, as Christian women of God, you must stand on the faith foundation that what God has for you is for you. If you feel deep down in your soul that there is more for you in life, you can feel confident in faith that your change is going to come, your deliverance is going to come, and your transformation is going to come.

The Apostle Paul wrote a series of letters to the Church of Corinth. The city of Corinth was a wealthy and popular city, much like Prince George's County, Maryland (where Ebenezer A.M.E. Church is located). Although it was commercially wealthy, there was another side to Corinth. It was a city of reckless and riotous living. The city of Corinth became synonymous with wealth, luxury, and immorality. Paul writes his letter in response to receiving word there was trouble in the Church of Corinth, and they needed his guidance. Likewise, Prince George's County with all of its affluent African American residents, positive attributes, and potential for greatness, has some issues. Like many other counties across the country, Prince George's County has experienced an increase in crime, drugs, and gang violence. Our public education system is in need of some changes. When we endeavor to change ourselves, God will give us the ability to change our community.

My sisters, if any woman be in Christ, she is a new creature. She is a new creation. She can't be the same. She has to change. She can't remain the same. The transformation must take place. When you become a new creation, old things must pass away. That means, we cannot allow there to be any drama in our new lives.

It is one thing to be with Christ. It is another thing to be in Christ and have the mind and heart of Christ. To be in Christ, we must love Him, love ourselves, and love each other. When we are in Christ, His spirit resides in us and we are new creatures in Him. We begin to grow in a new direction when Christ in us. Life becomes new and we are constantly changing as we begin to separate ourselves from worldly things and worldly pursuits. We receive a new nature, a new disposition, a new character, a new approach, a new attitude, and a new way of life. Our lives become extraordinary and we find that we are restored and ready. We begin to look at life differently.

My sisters, all of Heaven is waiting for your metamorphosis to occur. All of Heaven is waiting to see the new you. God has more for you. Hebrews 11:35-40, tells us that the clouds are full of female witnesses, who died without receiving the promise: "Women received back their dead, raised to life again. Others were tortured and refused to be released, so that they might gain a better resurrection. Some faced jeers and flogging, while still others were chained and put in prison. They were stoned; they were sawed in two; they were put to death by the sword. They went about in sheepskins and goatskins, destitute, persecuted and mistreated— the world was not worthy of them. They wandered in deserts and mountains, and in caves and holes in the ground. These were all commended for their faith, yet none of them received what had been promised. God had planned something better for us so that only together with us would they be made perfect."

My sisters, women are waiting for us to change. Big Momma, Auntie, and Nanna are waiting for us to yield. All we need to do is be willing to line up the vulnerable, weak places in our lives with the will of God and allow Him to make the shift and to transform us more into His image and His likeness.

Like the butterfly, we too have gone through various stages in life—from being an ordinary caterpillar, to becoming a hard-shelled chrysalis, to emerging as a unique and beautiful creature. I don't know about you, but I've endured some things in my life that caused me to develop a good hard shell, like the butterfly-in-waiting's chrysalis. When I got hurt, I isolated myself in my own cocoon. But there in that cocoon, in that time of separation and isolation, God called me to Himself and washed me and cleansed me with His blood. The transformation for the butterfly takes about two weeks. It may take two minutes, two hours, two days, two months, two years, or twenty years for your change to come. But one day your cocoon will open, and what went in looking old, ugly, and plain will emerge as a beautiful new thing. Old things will have passed away and all things will be new.

The transformation is the process of becoming a new woman, a new wife, a new Christian, a new mother, a new grandmother, a new auntie, a new co-worker, a new sister. It is getting to the place of reframing that occurs only after you have decided that there will be no more drama in your life. Once you have been transformed, God will begin a serious work on your behalf. He will bless those who bless you and curse those who curse you.

But you must choose to eliminate those things that produce drama in your life. From this day forward, you must choose to align your life with the will of God so that He can bless you beyond measure. I know this is true because I've watched God work a transformation miracle in my own life. Two weeks before I met my husband, Pastor Grainger Browning, I was feeling broken, hurt, and lonely. I decided I was going to line myself up with Jesus and it made no difference to me what the outcome would be. Two weeks later God gave me the desires of my heart.

I am a living witness for Christ. God has given me everything that I have desired, and I give Him all the glory. I had to go through my own transformation in order for things to pass away. I had to go back to the cross and see what Jesus did for me. I had to look in the empty tomb and see that He got up for me. I had to go to the upper room at Pentecost to see that I was in the room and that God gave me power. I had to make up in my mind that I wanted to change. And you've got to make up in your mind that you want to change.

It's time for you to make a promise to God that you will line yourself up with Him. Make the promise, and as you make the promise, decide to stop the drama that has been playing out in your life.

Reflections in Action

◆ The enemy uses drama and confusion to distract and deter us. Determine in your mind to stay focused on God no matter what you are going through.

◆ Pay attention to the people, places, and things that leave you feeling spiritually depleted. Those are the drama-inducers in your life. Get rid of them and get focused on God.

◆ Don't be afraid to change. A positive change in your life signifies growth, and you will need to be willing to grow and change if you want to walk with God.

◆ Don't allow other people's drama to filter into your life and cause problems where none existed previously.

◆ The best way for you to help a friend that is dealing with drama in her life is to pray with her and offer her scriptural edification.

◆ You must actively choose to live a drama-free life.

◆ Analyze your relationships so that you can recognize which ones help you as you grow towards God and which ones hinder your growth.

◆ Once God transforms you, do everything in your power to live your life according to His will.

◆ When God transforms you—tell somebody! Be a witness and help that sister realize that she can also live a life that is abundantly blessed and drama-free.

◆ Remind yourself daily that what God has for you is for you.

◆ Rest in the confident knowledge that your change will come.

Reflective Prayer

Father God,

Transform me, I need a change. I need Jesus to change my life to get me on track. I need a metamorphosis experience. I want the old things in my life to pass away and all things to become new for me. In this area right here, yes that one, right there! Transform those things in my life and my woman places that are hindering me from lining my life up with your will. I don't want to remain there anymore.

I want to change. I need a change. I am finished with that latest drama in my life. I need deliverance from my tendency for attracting drama. No more drama! No more drama! No more drama!

I've been going around this mountain long enough. Enough is enough. Please release me from unhealthy relationships, situations, and environments. Please relieve the pressure of taking care of others to the point that I have nothing left to take care of my own needs.

Please give me the strength to separate myself from that girlfriend who doesn't know how to be a friend, and send me a sister beloved, who will not abuse my kindness. Please give me the strength to separate myself from unhealthy relationships with men. I do not want the drama in my life anymore.

Father God, I want to be restored. I want to live a drama-free life that allows me to focus on you. I know that when the transformation process is over I will be ready to be who you ordained me to be. I'll be ready because I don't want any more drama in my life. In Jesus' name I pray.

Amen.

PART THREE

Ourselves ✤

10

What Has You Stuck?

As soon as they had brought them out, one of them said, "Flee for your lives! Don't look back, and don't stop anywhere in the plain! Flee to the mountains or you will be swept away!" By the time Lot reached Zoar, the sun had risen over the land. Then the Lord rained down burning sulphur on Sodom and Gomorrah—from the Lord out of the heavens. Thus he overthrew those cities and the entire plain, including all those living in the cities—and also the vegetation in the land. But Lot's wife looked back, and she became a pillar of salt.

(GENESIS 19:17, 23-26)

My sisters, I have an important question for you: What has you stuck? I have always been intrigued by the story of Lot's wife and why she looked back to Sodom and Gomorrah. As I read the story over and over again, I realized that a series of events unfolded that may have compelled her to look back. After all, Sodom and Gomorrah was her home. It was a place where she felt secure. It was the place where she got married and gave birth to her daughters. It was a sinful place, yet at the same time, her husband, Lot, chose Sodom and Gomorrah because it was rich in resources. The story of Lot's wife is full of contradictions, and to understand why she looked back, we need to examine them and retrace the events that led her to Sodom and Gomorrah.

The first contradiction occurs when Abram, his wife, Sarai, his nephew, Lot, and his father, Terah, left Ur of the Chaldeans and set out for Canaan, but when they reached Haran, they decided to settle there instead. My sisters, don't settle, when you know that God has something better up ahead for you. Do not stop at a point of convenience. Instead, press forward and get what God has ordained for you. In Genesis 12, the Lord told Abram to leave his country and his people and go to a new land. God promised Abram that He would make him into a great nation. God said He would bless those that bless him, curse those that curse him, and people on Earth will be blessed through him. So Abram, Lot, and their families left Haran.

The second contradiction occurs once they get to Egypt. Abram told Sarai not to tell people she was his wife. Sarai was very beautiful. Abram was worried that the Egyptians would kill him to have her. So he told Sarai to tell people that she was his sister. My sisters, there is no such thing as a little "white lie." There will come a time in all of our lives when we will have to face the consequences of our actions.

The third contradiction occurs in a much less obvious manner. As a result of Sarai's deception, Abram and Lot become wealthy. Abram received livestock, silver, and gold from Pharaoh who had fallen in love with his wife, Sarai. Pharaoh wanted to take Sarai to be his own wife. My sisters, you cannot get Godly blessings by ungodly means. When Pharaoh learned that Sarai was really Abram's wife, he banished them all from Egypt. When they settled in the land of Naggai, Abram and Lot's herdsmen began quarrelling because the land could not support all of them at the same time. In Genesis 13:8-9, Abram tells Lot: "Let's not have any quarreling between you and me, or between your herdsmen and mine, for we are brothers. Is not the whole land before you? Let's part company. If you go to the left, I'll go to the right; if you go to the right, I'll go to the left."

Here is the fourth contradiction: In Genesis 13:10, the Bible says, "Lot looked and saw the whole plain of Jordan and it was watered like the garden of the Lord or the garden of Eden, like the land of Egypt toward Zoar, which included Sodom and Gomorrah." How can a place that was so sinful have appeared so beautiful to Lot? My sisters, those old adages are true: All that glitters is not gold and the grass is not always greener on the other side.

Sodom and Gomorrah was a luscious place. It was irrigated by the river Jordan. It was fertile and it was breathtakingly beautiful. And when Lot chose it, he did so based on sight alone. There is no indication that Lot sought the Lord's guidance in his decision. His decision was provoked by what was visually appealing to him. My sisters, be careful about making decisions based on your sight alone. Although that man might look good to you on the outside, that does not give you an indication of what may be going on inside. Do not make a decision to enter into a relationship based solely on appearance.

Lot could not resist the lure of this green, fertile region. So he pitched his tent near Sodom. Initially he was not in Sodom; he was on the outskirts. Again my sisters, there is a lesson for us. Don't assume that because you are not fully immersed in a wicked situation that you won't eventually find yourself pulled all the way in. When you participate in "outskirt behaviors," you give the devil a foothold in your life. For example, you might not physically cheat on your spouse, but the fact that you have entertained the thought of adultery is an "outskirt behavior."

Lot chose the land because it was rich in resources. Lot might have thought that he was strong enough to resist the wickedness that characterized Sodom and Gomorrah. The people in Sodom and Gomorrah had no shame, no convictions, and no conscience. The men practiced homosexuality. In fact, the word "sodomy" was derived from Sodom. The people of Sodom and Gommorah did not know God. They did not fear Him and they did not respect His power or His might. The inhabitants of Sodom and Gomorrah had no boundaries. The lives were dictated and controlled by sin.

The Bible said the men of Sodom were sinning greatly against the Lord. In choosing this obviously wicked place, Lot turned his back on the fact that God had sustained him until this point. When Lot turned his back on God, he opened himself up to a life contrary to the will of God.

Here's the fifth contradiction: Lot came from the same family as Abram, yet there is no place in the scripture that says Lot asked God for direction. My sisters, have you ever thought about how you relate to God in comparison to your mother, your aunt, or your grandmother? Do you see a difference in how God works in the lives of his daughters who seek his guidance?

Lot fell prey to the enemy, and his decisions impacted his wife and his daughters. Genesis 13 ends with Abram, a man of faith, moving on as Lot parted from him. Abram sought God's guidance before making any decisions. And because Abram was faithful, God speaks blessings upon his life.

In Genesis 14:13, Abram finds out that all of Lot's possessions were seized by four kings. The Bible says that they took Lot and his possessions because Lot now lived in Sodom. When Abram heard his nephew had been captured, he pursued the army and recovered his nephew's wealth. King Melchizedek congratulates Abram on his victory, but Abram refuses to accept gifts from the king of Sodom. Abram was a man of great faith and he refused to accept gifts from a wicked man. My sisters, your actions and your faith must be in sync. It takes a tremendous amount of strength to deny the world's riches and stay true to God.

In Genesis 18:20-21 the Bible says, "the outcry against Sodom and Gomorrah is so great and their sin is so grievous that God heard the cries of Sodom and Gomorrah's victims; I will go down and see if what they have done is as bad as the outcry that has reached me. If not, I would know." God is getting ready to deal with the people of Sodom and Gomorrah.

God was concerned about the wickedness that was running rampant in the city of Sodom, and He was prepared to destroy the city. Abram tried unsuccessfully to intercede on behalf of the righteous people who lived in Sodom. God made up his mind about Sodom and Gomorrah. God shall not be mocked. My sisters, you cannot stay in sin and not end up in destruction. Through Jesus, we have the opportunity to escape destruction and sin.

In Genesis 19, God sends two male angels to the city to find out what is going on there. Lot insisted that the men stay at his house in order to prevent them from being raped by the men of Sodom and Gomorrah. My sisters, I want you to be very clear about this fact: Homosexuality is an abomination as is incest, adultery, promiscuity, and bestiality.

In Genesis 19, we see that although Lot had been present when Abram heard God's call, Lot decided to move to Sodom and Gomorrah and seek an easier life. He owned property in Sodom, he married his wife in Sodom, and he fathered two daughters in Sodom. Lot was not a bad man and neither was his wife. But, you cannot live your life surrounded by sin and expect that you won't be affected by it. In Genesis 19:6-8, Lot has become a pathetic, desperate, and broken man. He offers his own daughters to the rapists who had come for the angels. In doing so, Lot reduced himself and embraced the evilness of his surroundings at the expense of his daughters.

By this point, God has seen and heard enough. My sisters, God simply will not allow sin to reign supreme in your life. However, you can take comfort in the fact that once God decides to destroy the sin in your life, if you are faithful and do earnestly repent, He will give you a second chance.

Genesis 19:15 reads: "With the coming of dawn, the angels urged Lot, saying, 'Hurry! Take your wife and your two daughters who are here, or you will be swept away when the city is punished.'" Even though God was about to bring all of the darkness, evil, and sin of the past to an end, He was presenting Lot and his family with the opportunity for a new beginning.

My sisters, when God gives you an order to flee, Go! But, be sure you follow His divine instructions. When God brings you out of sin, you are to leave it alone forever. You are not to look back.

God's words are very clear to Lot and his family in Genesis 19:17: "As soon as they had brought them out, one of them said, "Flee for your lives! Don't look back, and don't stop anywhere in the plain! Flee to the mountains or you will be swept away!"

In the midst of all of the death, destruction, pain, and confusion, God was still merciful to Lot. My sisters, if you've ever thought to yourself that you did not deserve to be forgiven for your sins, let me remind you: God is merciful. The Bible says that God showed Lot favor and He allowed him to settle in the small town of Zoar. My sisters, your sin does not diminish God's love for you. If you repent and are heartily sorry for your misdoings, God will still show you favor.

After God frees them from sin, after He spares them from death, after He grants them forgiveness, and after He shows them favor, after their lives literally come full circle and God gives them a second chance, after all of that—Lot's wife looked back.

Why did she look back? Why, after all that God had done for her was she disobedient? To understand why she looked back, we must ask ourselves that same question: Why do we look back? After all that God has delivered us from, why are we disobedient? We, too, have heard God's commands and we, too, have ignored them.

What had her stuck? Was it the memories that compelled her, that compel us, to look back? Was it the fact that she didn't want to leave her family and friends that compelled her to look back? Was it just an emotional response? Did she just need one last look at the city where she was married and where she had birthed her children?

The Bible doesn't say she was a sinful woman. Lot's wife goes down in biblical history as the woman who looked back and turned to a pillar of salt. There's not much more that is said about her. In fact, the only other place she is recorded is in Luke 17:32, which reads, "Remember Lot's wife!" It is actually an admonishment. Luke reminds us what can happen to us when we look back.

My sisters, what Sodom and Gomorrah-like experiences has God delivered you from that you keep revisiting? What has you stuck? There are new blessings that God wants to pour out in your life, but you can't receive them because you are stuck on something in the past. You know you have been delivered from it, but the evil one keeps on pushing the rewind button in your mind. All those memories of regrets over past relationships or actions, bad decisions, and other sins of your past keep replaying in your mind. We find ourselves unable to press forward because we are still attached to the past pain, past problems, past issues, past sins, and we are stuck. Lot's wife, I do believe, if she had known the consequences, may not have looked back. But she did, and she became immobile; she became hard; she became cold; she became stuck; she became disconnected, and she died.

My sisters, God wants to deliver you from anything in your past that has you stuck because He has something better for you up ahead. It's time to relinquish the past and release the stagnation, fear, and all of your thoughts of unworthiness. It's time to reclaim your self-confidence and self-esteem.

There is no need for us to continue to carry the burden of our past sins. Jesus suffered, bled, died, and rose again for the remission of our past sins. That means all of your past mistakes have already been forgiven. Those past situations or circumstances have no power over you. Let them go and don't look back.

It is time to get ourselves "unstuck." If you are stuck, you know you are stuck, and God knows you are stuck. And He's waiting for you to confront your personal demons and move forward. There is nothing in your past that can prevent God from blessing you in the present.

It is time that we stop backing up from our purpose. The devil has been holding us hostage for too long, and the truth is that we've been willing hostages. We have given the enemy permission to keep rewinding our past. We've been willing participants in this hostage situation because we have not used the power that God has given us to rebuke the devil. We're just standing here, stuck in the muck of our past transgressions. We're just standing still, looking back and we've become cold, hard, brittle, and salty.

My sisters, in order to avoid becoming pillars of salt, we've got to learn how to affirm ourselves. If there is one way that the enemy gets us, it is because we're not always affirmed. As children, some of us were not told that we were beautiful, so we don't know how to feel good about ourselves, and the enemy beats us down. The lack of self-confidence and low self-esteem are common enemies to women. The tragedy of this type of mindset is that we pass our feelings of unworthiness on to our daughters, because our mothers experienced it and our grandmothers experienced it. We are the product of our history.

That history, coupled with our life experiences, gets combined, intermingled, and intertwined together, and we get stuck and feel unworthy. How in the world could we not be worthy? We were created in the image of God. We are fearfully and wonderfully made: worthiness is our birthright! Why do we feel unworthy? It's because of our Sodom and Gomorrah—it's because of our experiences.

Some of the sins that we have committed by thought, word or deed, are a direct response to our pain and our history. We must learn the art of self-affirmation and we must teach it to our daughters. We must learn how to look in the mirror, look ourselves in the eye, and give ourselves messages that affirm our worthiness:

✦ I am loving and worthy of love.
✦ I am strong and I am able.
✦ I am beautiful inside and out.
✦ My sins have been forgiven.
✦ My life has a purpose.
✦ I am blessed and I know it.
✦ I feel good about who I am and whose I am.
✦ I am a daughter of the Most High God.
✦ My past has passed.
✦ My future in God is certain.

You are fearfully and wonderfully made, but you've got to know it. Once we've learned how to affirm ourselves, we have to begin to affirm our sisters. Learn how to celebrate your sister's achievements. If you notice that she lost weight, tell her, affirm her. If you notice that she cut her hair, tell her, affirm her. When you see a sister who is making progress, tell her you've noticed and affirm her. As we affirm others, we affirm ourselves, and as we encourage others, we encourage ourselves.

My sisters, it's time to hold our heads up and start feeling great about ourselves and the things that God is doing in our lives. It's time we stop focusing on our imperfections and celebrate our worthiness. Stop telling yourself that your hips are too big, your hair is too short, your lips are too big, or your nose is too broad. We have been created in God's own image and I'm tired of us being stuck. We're moving forward and we're getting unstuck.

The scripture says the angels of God took Lot, his daughters, and his wife by the hand and pulled them out of Sodom just before God's wrath consumed the doomed city. Be an angel: If you see that your sister is headed down a path of destruction, take her hand and pull her out. Help your sister to get herself unstuck! Now, grab God's hand and pull yourself out. When God delivers you from your past, when God spares you from certain destruction, when He gives you favor and a second chance, no matter what you do—don't look back!

Reflections in Action

- When God gives you specific instructions and you understand them clearly—be obedient.

- Remember that we serve a loving, forgiving, and merciful God.

- Do not hesitate to ask God for His forgiveness, and in doing so, remember that God's favor does not diminish because we messed up. God gives us all second chances.

- Identify and list the things in your life that have you stuck and determine to get yourself unstuck.

- Recognize if you have low self-esteem and low self-confidence, and pray that God will restore these areas in your life, so that you can move forward with confidence and purpose.

- Remember Jesus carried the burden of your sins to the cross. Therefore those things that occurred in your past have been forgiven and you have been set free.

- Consciously let go of stuff that you can't fix or change.

- If the enemy keeps reminding you of your past mistakes, use your God-given authority to rebuke him and cast him back down to the pit of hell.

- Set your mind on heavenly thoughts of power, joy, peace, happiness, love, and prosperity.

- Look in the mirror and affirm yourself. Always know that you are worthy in the Lord's sight.

- Remember who you are in Christ and embrace the fact that you are fearfully and wonderfully made.

Reflective Prayer

Father God,

In the name of Jesus, I thank you that I am not stuck anymore. I am going to walk like the queen you made me to be and hold my head up. Devil, you can rewind that old tape all you want. It does not make a difference to me anymore. I put you under my feet; I cast you back into the pit of hell where you belong. Lord God, I will not look back and get stuck again. I am moving forward to where you want me to be.

I recognize that I have a past that in hindsight, I regret. I know I have not always done what you wanted me to do, and I ask for your forgiveness of my past actions.

I am ready to move forward in the things of God and to not look back on the past with questions or regret.

I put my past on the altar and I will rest in your divine plan for my life. I am truly grateful for another chance.

I give you the praise, Lord. I give you the glory. I give you the honor. I love you and thank you on this day. Thank you for your deliverance. In Jesus' name I want to say thank you. In Jesus' name I pray.

Amen.

11

Dressed to Kill

Finally, be strong in the Lord and in his mighty power. Put on the full armor of God so that you can take your stand against the devil's schemes. For our struggle is not against flesh and blood, but against the rulers, against the authorities, against the powers of this dark world and against the spiritual forces of evil in the heavenly realms. Therefore put on the full armor of God, so that when the day of evil comes, you may be able to stand your ground, and after you have done everything, to stand. Stand firm then, with the belt of truth buckled around your waist, with the breastplate of righteousness in place, and with your feet fitted with the readiness that comes from the gospel of peace. In addition to all this, take up the shield of faith, with which you can extinguish all the flaming arrows of the evil one. Take the helmet of salvation and the sword of the Spirit, which is the word of God. And pray in the Spirit on all occasions with all kinds of prayers and requests. With this in mind, be alert and always keep on praying for all the saints.

(EPHESIANS 6:10-18)

My sisters, have you ever been faced with something that makes you wonder if you can withstand the pressures of your reality? Have you ever felt like your situation or circumstance was simply more than you could bear? If you have, I want you to know that you are not alone. All of God's daughters find themselves challenged at different times along the journey. But our Father does not let us get lost in the wilderness. Through His Word in the Book of Ephesians, God has provided the tools for us to stand up and conquer the very things in life that threaten to overtake us when we have to confront them.

The Book of Ephesians is a collection of letters that the apostle Paul wrote to the church at Ephesus. The theme of Ephesians is to help Christians to understand the eternal purpose and power of God. This letter to the church at Ephesus states that evil is a reality. The sole purpose of the enemy is to seek, kill, and destroy God's chosen people. My sisters, you need to acknowledge the fact that evil exists and it wants to devour and to denounce the divine order of God. As women of God, we need to know that we cannot oppose evil—only God can oppose evil. But the good news is that Jesus the Christ gave us power to overcome evil when He died, was buried, rose, and ascended into Heaven. There are four charges to the church in the letters to the church at Ephesus:

1. to promote unity within the church
2. to renounce unchristian ways
3. to build up Christian faith and hope in the lives of families
4. to put on the whole armor of God to fight against the reality of evil

My sisters, the fourth charge speaks directly to us. It is time to get dressed to kill and to destroy the enemy. In spiritual warfare, you cannot rely upon your own strength. When you find yourself engaged in battle with evil forces, you have to call upon the strength of the Lord. You must be strong in the things of God: you must be saved, you must know the Word, you must know how to pray, you must know how to worship, and you must offer God praise.

There are powers, spirits, and authorities that are all fighting against the plan of God. You cannot negate the reality of evil. Our experiences, our journeys, our walk confirms that there is an active power of evil in the world. For example, the delay in response to victims of Hurricane Katrina is an example of pure evil at work. The local, state, and federal governments knew that Katrina was on its way. Yet they did nothing. As a result, intentional or unintentional, thousands died. That was evil, pure and simple.

We experience evil in our workplaces. We see it at work in our relationships. We have come face to face with evil in our daily struggles with our sinful natures. It's time for us to put our gear on, to get dressed to kill and destroy the enemy's plans for us. He wants us to live a defeated life. In order to defeat his evil plans for us, we have to fight. We're not going out without a battle. So get your full armor on.

We can't go into battle half dressed. Before we can fight against the evil one, we must put on the full armor of God. Paul confirms the reality that the devil does have power. The only way we can destroy the enemy's schemes and plans is to fight him dressed in the full armor of God. This is warfare. We need the suit and the weapons that God supplies for us to fight effectively.

What Paul said in the first century is still true in the twenty-first century. There is a reality of demonic power at work that is impacting and influencing human affairs. There is wickedness in the heavenly places. Evil does exist. We see it at work in our government. We see it at work in corporate America. We see it at work in our school systems. We even see it at work in the church. As women of God, we cannot walk around blind to the reality that evil is trying to destroy us. We've got to get dressed to kill.

The first thing you've got to do after you've made up your mind that you are going to fight is stand firm. No matter how scared you may be, you have to stand flat-footed against evil. So we need to get fully dressed, because evil inevitably will come. When it comes, we need to have our full armor on so that we can stand. But we've got to do more than just stand, we've got to be able to withstand the evil things that will come against us. We've got to be overcomers in order to be victorious. This is a real fight we're in, and the only way to win is to get dressed in the full armor of God.

In Ephesians, Paul names the six elements that comprise the full armor of God:

1. belt of truth
2. breastplate of righteousness

3. shoes
4. shield
5. helmet
6. sword

The belt of truth. We must belt ourselves with truth. What does that mean? It means we must undergird ourselves with what is godly and what is righteous. Roman soldiers belted themselves. In fact, they wore a belt and they had a sword. When they put the belt on, the sword hung in a separate piece attached to the belt that allowed the soldiers to move freely. My sisters, when you live as a Christian, there is no reason for you to have to guess or to grope with what is right. That's what sinners do. Those of us who wear the belt of truth know what to do. With the belt of truth, you can determine your next defensive move in this spiritual battle. It's time to get dressed. Put your belt on.

The breastplate of righteousness. The breastplate of righteousness covers the breast area. When you have it firmly in place you will know that you are living a life that is upright and pleasing in the sight of God. It's time to get dressed. Put your breastplate on.

Shoes. Your feet must be fitted with the readiness that comes from the gospel of peace. In other words, you have got to be equipped and ready to move. You have to be ready to respond with peace in the midst of the battle. My sisters, in the battle, you don't become the hell raiser. You don't start pulling off your earrings and putting Vaseline on your face. You don't start scratching up anybody's car, or putting sugar in the tank, or cursing people out. You must walk in the role of the peacemaker. You must take the high road. It's like my momma says: "Don't wallow in dirt." It's time to get dressed. Put your shoes on.

The shield of faith. For a Roman soldier, the shield was the key weapon in battle. Paul uses this metaphor to help us understand that our faith in God protects us from Satan's fiery darts. The Roman soldier's shield was very large. Its shape was oblong and it was made of wood with two sections glued together. The whole thing was covered with leather that protected the soldier's whole body. Back then, the soldiers had to ward off darts with fire on the end. When the darts hit the oblong shield, they sank into the wood and leather, and the flame was extinguished.

My sisters, our faith in God can literally extinguish the fiery darts of the enemy. Because we have faith, we can tell when the enemy has launched his fiery darts in our direction. We know what evil looks like and what it feels like. Because our faith enables us to recognize evil, we know that God can change it, snuff it out, and get rid of it. God can heal our bodies, He can turn our situations around, and He can cause a shift in our circumstances. God can stop the madness. He provides for us and He makes ways for us. No matter what you need God to do for you—change your job, pour out blessings, give you the desires of your heart, work a miracle, give you a sign—whatever you stand in need of, God can do it! It's time to get dressed. Get your shield.

The helmet of salvation. Now, the helmet of salvation that Paul is referring to is not only knowing we are saved, but that we are forgiven of our sins of the past. In the battle of life, when we are dressed to kill with our helmet of salvation on, we have the power to face sin in life and call it out for what it is and know that when we are saved, we can overcome sin. When we put on our helmet of salvation, we are also reminded of who we are and whose we are. My sisters, when you realize that you are a force against evil through Christ who lives in you, you can feel empowered and confident in the fight. It's time to get dressed. Put your helmet on.

The sword of the spirit. My sisters, this is one of the mightiest weapons we have at our disposal. The sword of the spirit is the Word of God. It is our principal weapon of defense. It is the choice weapon to use against sin. We cannot win our battles with the enemy without the Word of God. The Word is the utterance God gives us in order to fight and win. For example, in Luke 12:12, Jesus says, "for the Holy Spirit will teach you at that time what you should say." Whatever battles we may find ourselves engaged in, we need to know that God will give us the right words to speak. Have you ever found yourself replaying an incident in your mind that left you thinking, "I should've said this or I should've said that?" And then later, you realize that if you had said this or that, your situation would have been even worse? Thank God for divine utterances. Not only will

God give you scripture, but God will tell you what to say and how to say it so that it will make the difference in your situation.

Some of you think that quoting scripture is the only thing you can do. But if you are connected with God, He will speak a word to you for you to speak in a certain way, with a certain tone, that will make the difference in your situation. Read the Word daily, meditate on it, and make it a part of your everyday life. It's time to get dressed, sisters. Get your sword!

Now that we are dressed to kill and ready to go into this battle, there is one more thing that we need to do before we march on to the battlefield. We must pray. The greatest weapon of all is prayer. Paul says three things about prayer:

1. *It must be constant and consistent.* Don't just pray when you're facing a crisis. We must pray daily to get the strength we need to fight. Daily prayers can strengthen us before the battle, during the battle, and after the battle.
2. *It must be intense and intentional.* In other words, we must pray concentrated, intentional prayers. Our prayers must consist of more than a limp recital of the Lord's Prayer. Our prayers must be specific, fervent prayers. Talk to God. Tell Him what you need. It's time that we start speaking specific prayers to God, with the faith that He hears us. And if what we want is in His will for us, He will answer.
3. *It must be unselfish and unassuming.* We must learn how to be intercessors for others and not have our prayers always be focused on our own issues. So as we pray for the strength to fight our own battles, we must also pray for the strength of others in their battles.

My sisters, you may not be facing a battle right now, but rest assured, you will. But as long as you prepare yourself to fight by putting on the full armor of God, you will not need to waste a minute worrying about the enemy's plans for you.

Remember your armor. Take it with you everywhere you go. I am convinced that the devil wants to destroy us in every facet of our lives. I'm particularly convinced of this as it pertains to women. We constantly have to prove ourselves. Women are just about on the bottom of everything: We are the lowest wage earners, we are not as fit as we should be, and we die of breast cancer at a rate that is higher than any other sickness. I know it's the plan of the devil. Satan knows that we are givers of life. So, if he can wipe us out, the generation of God's people will not continue.

There is a difference in how we are treated. For example, I was in Atlanta visiting family. When I'm in a hotel, I always leave a tip for the housekeeper. I write a note that says, "Thank you and God bless." This is something I do every time I travel. I bless my sister, no matter if she's black, white, or Latina. That housekeeper is my sister.

Well, just when I was leaving the money, my son, GT called. I was racing around the room gathering my things, because I had a flight to catch, but a mother always has time for her son. As I was talking to him, I left the note, left the money, left the room, took my key, put it in the express checkout box, rolled my suitcase out, and went downstairs to hail a cab. When I opened my purse, I realized that I had left my wallet in my room. I ran back up the stairs. I tried to get my key from the checkout box, but I could not.

I ran back down to the lobby. The woman behind the desk asked if she could help me. I told her what happened. She said, "I need your ID." I gave it to her, and in doing so, I couldn't help but wonder at her total lack of sensitivity, understanding, and compassion for my predicament.

She should have called security or walked back to the room with me. Instead, she offered me no help at all. She looked at my ID and very slowly gave me another key. I ran to the elevator. When I got to the room, my wallet was right on the desk where I had forgotten it. So I thanked the Lord. Then I went back to the lobby to see her.

I said, "I have my wallet, and here is your key. And, I need to say this to you so that the next time someone is in a crisis, and she looks like me, respond as if she were a white man." She was speechless. I told her, "If I were a white man, you would have called security; you would have handled this differently. But I want you to know that a crisis is a crisis, no matter if it's a black woman or a white man, so I need to educate you. Anytime a patron of this hotel is in a crisis, regardless of what he or she looks like, you should respond quickly with compassion and sensitivity. In other words, respond as if the patron were a white man." With that said, I added, "God bless you," and I walked away.

Do you understand what I'm saying? Do the words on this page resonate in your life? Nobody knows what women endure, except another woman. Your children don't know and your significant other or husband doesn't know. Only we walk in these shoes. I don't care if you're black, white, Asian, or Latina... we share a collective experience as women. But we can endure it all, as long as we're dressed to kill. Get your full armor on!

Reflections in Action

+ In your battles in life, sometimes simulating getting dressed for the battle and dealing with the reality of the enemy opens the door to your breakthrough.

+ Stand up.

+ If you have a belt on, take it off. If not, act like you are taking off your belt.

+ Now, put your belt on. Put it back on.

+ Now, if you have a jacket, take it off. If you don't have a jacket, act like it. Put your breastplate on.

+ Now, take your shoes off.

+ Put your shoes back on.

+ Now, if you have a hat, put your hat on.

+ Now, get your faith shield and draw it up in front of you.

+ Cover yourself all the way up.

+ Get your sword, get your Bible, get your Bible, get your Bible.

+ Now start praying. Pray for your sister and pray for yourself.

+ You've won the battle, you've won the battle, you've won the battle.

+ Now get on your knees and verbally rebuke the enemy out of your situation.

+ Believe in faith that you will be victorious.

Reflective Prayer

Father God,

I thank you and praise you. Great and mighty you are to me. Wonderful and marvelous you are to me. Savior you are to me. Deliverer you are to me. Healer you are to me. I say thank you. Thank you for being God, and God all by yourself. Now God, in the name of Jesus, do what you need to do. I bless your name and thank you for what you've done for me thus far along my journey of faith.

From this day forward, every time that I have to confront the reality of the devil in my life, I will go into the battle with the right equipment and the right attire in the spirit realm. I'm looking good in the natural, but in the spiritual, I am dressed to kill the devil and all his cohorts, his imps, his demons, his witches, his warlocks, his jezebels, his harlots, and his whores.

I come not shrinking or feeling fearful, but I come with boldness and your Holy Ghost power.

I know that the enemy is a roaring lion that wants to kill, steal, and destroy. But I also know that you are the King of Kings and the Lord of Lords and that you have all power to defeat the enemy.

Ultimately, I know that the battle is not mine, but yours. As I put my spiritual war gear on and get fully "Dressed to Kill," I place everything in your hands.

I thank you in the name of Jesus the Christ that the battle is won in the spirit realm, and I know in faith that it shall be won in the earthly realm. And so I thank you and I praise you for the belt of truth, the breastplate of righteousness, for my feet that are shod with the gospel of peace, for the shield of faith, for the helmet of salvation, and for my sword—the Word of God. In Jesus' name I pray.

Amen.

12

Bag Lady

So God created man in his own image, in the image of God he created him; male and female he created them.

(GENESIS 1:27)

My sisters, the time has come for us to open ourselves up and embrace that which God has called us to be. It's time to occupy the places that God has ordained for us individually and collectively. This is going to be a journey of faith, and you must consent to travel with God. If we do not open up, we will miss what God has set aside for us. This journey will not end on this side of glory. The journey of faith will continue until you reach God's Kingdom in Heaven, and your reward will reflect the way you journeyed in the flesh.

It is time that you understand that if you need God to do something for you, and you are in a right relationship with Him through Christ, He will do it. You have got to be sure of the things you want from God, because if you are certain, and you're living your life in accordance to God's will, and you sincerely want what God wants to give you, He will give it to you. And, my sisters, you want to be ready when God moves in your life. It's time to open yourself up for the move of God in your life.

All of us must be able to see ourselves doing the thing we were created to do. All of us need to see ourselves living out our purpose in service to God and His people. God created each one of us for a specific purpose that will ultimately help to bring about the Kingdom of God.

But before we can continue on this journey of faith, we must embrace who we are and whose we are. We need to be able to see the reflection of God in our women places. Genesis 1:27 reads, "So God created man in his own image, in the image of God he created him; male and female he created them."

We are divinely created in the very image of God. Therefore, we should strive to reflect God in our spirit, because God is spirit. I challenge you to take charge of your spirit and align your life with God's will. Women of God, we need to consciously reach for God through Jesus Christ. We need to be in sync with God. We need to be responsive to God. We need to be rigorous in God. Most importantly, we need to rest in God. We need to be able to rest in His will, His ways, and His word. To accomplish all of this, once we reach for God and grab hold of Him, it is our responsibility to stay the course. I am a living witness that this is definitely easier said than done, because we have a natural tendency to get off track when we are faced with the realities of life.

My sisters, on this journey of faith we can find ourselves in some compromising positions. We often find ourselves in situations where we did not do what Jesus would have done. We must admit that. We knew that what we were doing was wrong, but we did it anyway.

God is telling us that we need to relinquish some things. We need to let go of some things. We need to extricate ourselves from those relationships that we know are displeasing to God. God is telling us that it is time for us to simply let some things go.

Remember Erykah Badu's song *Bag Lady*? So many of us are walking around like the sister she sang about—bent over, with our backs almost broken from all of the unnecessary junk and excess baggage that we've been carrying around. On the journey of faith, there is no room for excess baggage. We must let it go.

Some of you are reading this and thinking to yourselves "Erykah who?" but, don't be so holy that you can't identify. In her song,

Sister Badu actually names the baggage handlers: There's the garbage bag lady, the Gucci bag lady, and the nickel bag lady, among others. Which bag lady are you? What junk is weighing you down? What bad habits are stifling your growth?

By relinquishing our past, we can repent and resume our intimate relationship with God. The Book of Second Chronicles 7:14 reads, "If my people, who are called by my name, will humble themselves and pray and seek my face and turn from their wicked ways, then will I hear from Heaven and will forgive their sin and will heal their land." My sisters, we are on a journey of faith and we have got to let go of some things.

God requires us to humble ourselves and pray. He requires us to seek His face and turn from our evil ways. We must initiate the transformative power of God in our lives. God is looking for us to do something. We humble ourselves when we let go and say to God, "I yield, I give in, I don't want to do this thing anymore."

When you let go of your baggage, you will notice that when you reach for the things of God, you will be able to make contact because all of your mess is out of the way. What seemed unattainable to you, when you were carrying all of your bags, will now be attainable. When we are unencumbered by our baggage, we can get in sync with God. We can go with the flow and move of God in any situation.

We need to submit our will to God in such a way, that if God says, "go left," we go left. If God says, "go right," we go right. If God says, "stand still," we stand still. If God says, "back up," we back up. When we are truly in sync with God, there is an absence of fear, doubt, or concern. When our will is intertwined with God's will, we are then able to move with the flow of God.

God wants us to be wrapped in Him, so that we can respond to His call and purpose for our lives without reservation. When we wrap ourselves up in God, we can hear Him as He speaks into our lives. We can expect that His promises to us will come to pass, and we can rest while we wait for Him to move.

When we reach this level of relationship with God, the desire to please God with our whole heart, soul, and mind becomes our primary goal. This means we cannot allow our baggage to discourage us. We cannot let anything get in the way or stop us from doing God's will. We cannot allow anybody or anything to disappoint us, distract us, or deter us. When God calls, we are to respond rigorously.

My sisters, whether you realize it or not, you have had the benefit of learning from the women who have journeyed ahead of you and paved the way for you. The time has come for us to pave the way for the young women who are coming behind us.

You cannot stay in the same place, doing the same thing for 2000 years until you die. You must mentor another sister, so that one day she can step into her place. You may need to re-read that sentence. I know some of you are thinking that I'm suggesting that you set another sister up to take "your place." That's not it at all. I'm encouraging you to help her be prepared to step into her destiny. You might know a young woman who is in the same profession as you. Or you might know a new mother or a new wife who could benefit from your wisdom. The lessons you've learned along the way can help her. God is ordering us to reach out to younger women to mentor them, help them, share our experiences with them, encourage them, and pray for them.

For example, I used to run relay races. When you run relay, after you finish your lap, you must hand off the baton. When you pass the baton, your aim must be accurate. You must pass it to the next runner in one precise and skillful moment. If you pass it too early, you will cause the next runner to have to overextend herself and break her stride. If you pass it too late, you will cause the next runner to run harder and faster than necessary. But when you pass it at the precise moment, the next runner can receive it and run with it.

Now, the person who is receiving the baton has to be in the right position. You have to be focused and ready to run when the baton hits your palm. You can't be distracted by the crowd. You've got to be in position, looking toward the goal, looking toward the end, looking to the finish line, and expecting to win. Stay in your position. Wait for the hand-off. The fastest runner on the team is always the last runner. My sisters, the truth is that some of us just don't run as fast as we used to. We need to pass the baton to some younger, faster women of God.

We must mobilize a new generation. We must build young women up, so that they can move forward. We must enable our gifted, talented, and anointed young women to do what it is that

God is calling them to do. We must live as examples, so that these young women will see us and want to draw closer to the very things of God. We must help them to be confident in the fact that they have been created in His image. In order to show our younger sisters how to see themselves, we must see ourselves as God sees us, and not as the world sees us.

In the book, *See Yourself as God Sees You,* author Josh McDowell writes, "the way to know that we are in God and what contributes to our identity, we must [first] deal with who we are not. For although we know that we are created in His image, we let the journey of life decide to create and define our identity." In my own journey of faith, I noticed that there are three major myths that have added to our collective problem of not being able to see ourselves the way God sees us.

+ *Myth #1: We identify ourselves by our outward appearance.*
For many of us, our outward appearance is everything. We constantly need someone to validate that we look good. We formulate our views on our appearance so much that we get depressed if people do not compliment us. We look good outside, but we are dying inside. In First Samuel 16:7, Samuel went looking for the king: "But the Lord said to Samuel, 'Do not consider his appearance or his height, for I have rejected him. The Lord does not look at the things man looks at. Man looks at the outward appearance, but the Lord looks at the heart.'" So, let's debunk that myth right now. You need to know in your heart that you are God's unique creation. Your value and worth are infinite. Who you are is not determined by your outward appearance. God defines who you are by looking at your heart. As Christian women with a purpose and responsibility in the Kingdom of God, our consciousness of who we are must be raised. We have been victims of our history, or should I say our *herstory.* Our herstory has prevented us from effectively stepping into our ultimate purpose. God is calling us forth to take our rightful place. God is ordering those of us who are caught up in outward appearances to release that baggage—let it go.

◆ *Myth #2: You are what you do.* In other words, our performance determines our self worth. As women, we often look for
affirmation in the things we do. You only feel good when
someone acknowledges you for putting the program together,
or for organizing the event, or because you obtained a partic-
ular position or office. If you are doing what you do just so
that others will acknowledge you, then you may be basing
your identity on your performance instead of your infinite
worth to God. You need to separate your sense of self-worth
from your accomplishments. When Jesus selected the 12 dis-
ciples, He called them first to be with Him, and then He sent
them out to preach. My sisters, on this journey of faith, we
must get our priorities straight. It is not what you do that
determines your identity. Your relationship with God through
Jesus Christ is the determining factor. Therefore, it is critical
that we understand and embrace the blessed reality we belong
to God first and foremost. The Lord has to be in His rightful
place in your life. Your accomplishments cannot mean more
to you than living a life that is pleasing before God.

◆ *Myth #3: You are somebody only if you have power.* There
are those of us who feel good about ourselves because we
have power, influence, and control over others. We are
wrapped up in our status. We are driven to seek position,
not to please God. We will say and do anything to gain
position. The Bible is clear that our identity, as God's
creation, does not depend upon our position in the world.
In Matthew 23:11-12 (KJV), Jesus said, "But he that is
greatest among you shall be your servant. And whosoever
shall exalt himself shall be abased; and he that shall humble
himself shall be exalted." So my sisters, you do not have to
pursue position, just let God do what He does. If you were
meant to have position, then it will be so. You will not have
to do anything. Let God do it. If you humble yourself, the
Lord will exalt you. It does not matter whether you have
position or power, or whether you achieve great things or
small. What matters is that you have a healthy sense of self-
esteem. You have to see yourself as God sees you.

We must transcend these myths, misconceptions, and misunderstandings, so that we can move into a refreshing, revitalizing relationship with God. If we don't, we will stunt our growth and delay our purpose in the Kingdom of God.

It's time to yield to God. It's time to surrender and commit to Him. If we would only commit, God will remove the things that are blocking us from Him. Consider the story of Lazarus (John 11:38-44). In order to get to Lazarus, Jesus had the stone that was blocking the entrance to the tomb removed. Metaphorically speaking, Jesus has also removed the stone for those of us who are saved and have accepted Christ. We, like Lazarus, have become deadened along the journey. We need Jesus to give us new life and a fresh anointing. When Jesus called Lazarus forth from the grave, Lazarus emerged with his hands and feet bound, his grave clothes still on, and a napkin over his head. In John 11:44, Jesus said to those gathered, "Take off the grave clothes and let him go."

There is a process that we all must go through to become who God wants us to be. There is a process on the journey in evolving into the woman that God desires you to be. When we become Christians, we receive new life, but, like Lazarus, we often emerge from our past life wearing spiritual grave cloths. My sisters, Jesus is calling your name. He is calling you to come forth so that He can loose those things that have had you bound and set you free.

My parents got divorced when I was six years old. I was the oldest child, and I felt like I was the one who had to take care of my mother and brother. Although my daddy lived in walking distance, I still felt responsible for them. The truth is, even though my intentions were good, my misplaced sense of responsibility had me bound.

I lived my whole life saved, but still wearing my grave clothes. Then one year while I was facilitating a workshop at a women's conference, God revealed the negative influence that my childhood experience was having on my life, my marriage, my mothering, my ministry, and my identity. Jesus called me to come forth. He needed to loose me, so that I could become the woman God had destined me to be. When I relinquished the hold that my past had on me, I saw my true identity. I saw who I was in Jesus Christ, and I began to walk confidently in my purpose. I began to move in a place in God that

He had desired for me all along. I could minister freely to other women and be a witness without reservation.

God did not intend for us to live our lives bound, wearing grave clothes, and dragging our heavy baggage behind us. He wants to free us up and move us to the next level in His Kingdom on Earth as it is in Heaven. In order to find your true identity, you must allow God to unwrap you. Ask Him to reveal to you what needs to be peeled away, so that you can see yourself as God sees you, and you can get the most out of life. Refer to the following scriptures often, especially when you need to be reminded just how great God is:

+ PSALM 139:1-6. God is all-knowing. He knows all about our past, He knows all about our present, and He already knows about our future. He can bring good out of the worst situation.
+ PSALM 139:7-10. God is everywhere. There is not a place in Heaven or on Earth where God can't find you.
+ PSALM 31:5. God is truth. He cannot lie.
+ MALACHI 3:6. God is unchangeable. He is not fickle and moody like us. You can depend on God.
+ PSALM 33:4. God is faithful. You can trust God to do what He said He is going to do.
+ FIRST PETER 1:15-16. God is Holy. The moves that He makes in your life will be lined up with His holy characteristics. Our God is an awesome God.

This is key: God wants us to let go of our baggage and remove our grave clothes so that our minds, hearts, and spirits can be stayed on Him. We need to redefine our mindset: It's no longer my thing; it's God's thing. It's no longer about what I want; it's all about what God wants.

Ask God to give you the strength to drop your bags. I don't know if it's a past marriage or relationship that has you bound and is preventing you from opening your heart to someone else. If so, drop that bag. Focus on the facts: The brother is gone—move on. He messed up—move on. Or perhaps you're carrying your children as baggage: Your children are 25 or 30 years old and still living in your house.

It's time to tell those adults to get a job, stand on their own two feet, and move on. Move on. You may be carrying the baggage of your past sins: There are things that you might have done in the past that the enemy is still using to bind and torture you. The devil is a liar. God can set you free immediately so that you can move on.

Some of you may not be carrying any baggage at all; some of you may still be wearing your grave clothes. You've moved past the relationship, you've encouraged your grown kids out of your house, you've overcome your past, but you're still bound. You love God; you're saved, sanctified, Holy Ghost filled, and fire baptized, but you are still living a defeated life because you are walking around in your grave clothes. You can't praise God. You can't lift your hands up to worship Him. When the preacher says give the Lord some praise, you have a hard time praising Him. You need to come out of your grave clothes. The spirit of oppression and depression must flee, in the name of Jesus.

My sisters, the time has come for us to make a change. It's time for us to consent to move with God. A new generation is relying on us to get it right and pass our knowledge on to them. There is no time to be bogged down with thoughts of pleasing the world. Let God release you from your past. Ask Him to unwrap you. And when He does—and He will—drop your bags immediately!

Reflections in Action

✦ Get the thing you know that you need to let go of in the fore-front of your mind and spirit. It may be a bad relationship or it may be bad habits (drinking, smoking, lying, or gossiping) or it may be even worse. Whatever it is, get it in the forefront of your mind, open your mouth, and shout "God I give it to you!"

✦ And after you shout, release it.

✦ Look in the mirror and speak these affirmations to yourself:

◇ I am blessed in the heavenly realm with every spiritual blessing.

◇ I was chosen before the creation of the world to be holy.

◇ I have been redeemed by the blood of Jesus.

◇ I am forgiven, I am forgiven, I am forgiven.

◇ I am sealed with the Holy Spirit.

◇ Jesus died to set me free.

✦ Find a piece of clothing that you no longer wear because it's old, out of style, or too big. Choose anything that reflects the "old you." Put it on, look at yourself, and revel in that fact that these grave clothes are no longer right for you.

✦ Find a young woman to mentor, either through your church, through your company, or someone you've noticed along the way.

✦ Lovingly help another sister recognize her baggage. Sometimes we can't see the bags we're carrying.

✦ Make sure you are not living under the myths that have caused so many sisters to lose sight of God.

Reflective Prayer

Father God,

I thank you for creating me in your image. I thank you that my will is intertwined with your will. God, I am releasing my issues unto you. My past is not going to hold me hostage any longer. My insecurities will no longer dictate how I will live my life. I surrender all to you. I give all of my unhealthy relationships to you.

Like Lazarus, I want to take off my grave clothes. I do not want anything to get in the way of having an intimate relationship with you. Please loose the bindings. Lord God, please remove those things that have kept me from moving forward into another place in you.

I want to be transformed and changed. I want to be how you want me to be, God. I realize that you have pre-ordained a purpose for me that is beyond anything I could ever possibly think or imagine.

I can feel you doing something new in me. You are removing the stone. I can shed my grave clothes and drop my bags. I can have a new and everlasting life in you.

You have called me to do a work. I want to use the gifts and talents you have blessed me with in service to you. I thank you that you have blessings with my name on them stored up for me. I am ready to receive them. Now that I have dropped my bags, my hands are free for me to raise towards Heaven. Lord God, rain down your blessings upon me.

I want to live right, I want to do right, and I want to walk right. I want to be a blessing to somebody else. I want to mentor someone. I want to be able to share. I want to be able to deposit into someone's life the things of God. I want to be bold in you. I want to be obedient and faithful to you, no matter what. God, just take this thing off me, set me free, set me free, Lord, set me free. In Jesus' name I pray.

Amen.

13

A Good Cry

Thus saith the LORD of hosts, Consider ye, and call for the mourning women, that they may come; and send for cunning women, that they may come: And let them make haste, and take up a wailing for us, that our eyes may run down with tears, and our eyelids gush out with waters. For a voice of wailing is heard out of Zion, How are we spoiled! We are greatly confounded, because we have forsaken the land, because our dwellings have cast us out. Yet hear the word of the LORD, O ye women, and let your ear receive the word of his mouth, and teach your daughters wailing, and every one her neighbour lamentation.

(JEREMIAH 9:17-20 KJV).

As women who were created in God's image, we are wrapped up in Him and He is wrapped up in us. In creating women, God poured both sides of Himself—His strength and His sensitivity—into the core of our very being. As young girls we are raised to be "ladylike" and to reflect God's compassionate, sensitive, and nurturing side. We are taught that we are supposed to be the embodiment of God's soft side, His tender side.

Although we have also been endowed with God's strength, the female side of His image calls us to be nurturing in our strength and in our influence and to love others unconditionally. Generally, we tend to show our sensitive side to the world because it is what most identifies us as women. But oftentimes, life has dictated that we compensate and identify with our stronger self, that side of us that must step up when we have no other choice but to be strong.

Those of you who are single mothers have had to be both mother and father to your children. You have no choice but to play a dual role in raising your children: you have to be mommy-soft to console them and daddy-strong to confront them. You have to have it together at all times. There may have been times when you were so physically tired and emotionally worn out from your dual responsibilities that all you wanted to do was sit down and have yourself "a good cry." But you wanted your kids to see you being strong—there was no time for tears.

You may hold a position of corporate leadership that a woman has never held. Day in and day out, you have to assert yourself and constantly prove that you have what it takes to lead. You have had to push your sensitive side down and allow the strong side to take over, just to make it through. There were times you wanted to close your corner office door, go into your private executive washroom, and have yourself a good cry. But you couldn't let them see that the pressure and the on-the-job difficulties were beginning to take their toll on you—there was no time for tears.

My sisters, it is critically important that you rediscover, restore, reclaim, resurrect and reconnect with your sensitive side. It is the essence of your womanhood, and it has been oppressed, tucked away, and hidden deep under the covers of life. Your sensitive side has been lying dormant for too long. It's time to release the pain, the disappointments and the grief. It's time to cleanse your heart and soul from the inside out. It's time to have yourself "a good cry."

God is calling forth the weeping and the wailing women. Your victory and healing will be released in the flow of your tears, and you will never be the same again. When life forces us to push our sensitive side down, we can become angry, bitter, indifferent, mean-spirited and insensitive. When we reach this state, the level of sensitivity and compassion that once characterized us as women has been severely diminished. We need to reclaim it.

God is calling forth the weeping and the wailing women. Perhaps you have endured a terrible divorce and the pain and the loss was so devastating that you vowed never to trust another man again. Perhaps you have never been married, but you opened yourself up to someone, and because he broke your heart into a million pieces, you think you are incapable of love. Or maybe your husband was unfaithful, or maybe you lost a loved one, or maybe you suffered a miscarriage, or you had an abortion.

Perhaps you were raped or violated by incest or rejected by a parent. Maybe your best friend betrayed you. I'm calling out every demon, so that sins you have committed can no longer oppress you; so that the regrets you have can no longer plague you; and, so the hurts you suffered can no longer haunt you. Stop replaying the past over and over in your mind—you cannot change it. It's time you had yourself "a good cry." Let the Lord do the work through your tears.

Cry so that you can move on! Cry so that you can claim the victory! Cry so that you can function as a woman of God like never before! You need to face the hurt, face the pain, face the experiences and allow yourself to have a good cry so that you can be whole again.

God wants you to indulge in a good cry so that you can press towards the mark of the high calling and go and claim what belongs to you. When you don't allow God to heal you, you will find yourself trapped in an emotional stronghold. When you shut down your emotions, you end up living outside of what God has ordained for your life.

Are you constantly complaining? Do you become irritated for no apparent reason? Are you often annoyed? Do you frustrate easily? Do you frequently suffer from discontent? These negative feelings can take root in the hurt and pain that result when you are out of sync with your sensitive side.

God wants to restore the balance in your life. Give Him your tears and He will wash away every pain that inhabits your heart. God's gift of tears can wash away the pain, the hurt, the disappointment and the regret and restore, replenish and resurrect balance in your life.

In Jeremiah 9:17-20, the prophet records God's call for the weeping and wailing women, the professional mourners. Their job was to get the bereaved and others at a funeral to cry properly, to go through the grieving process in order to deal with their loss and devastation. God calls the women to wail, to cry, and to weep for His people. But perhaps most importantly, God tells the women to teach others, especially their daughters, how to cry.

It is imperative that women reclaim and get restored in the place where love, sensitivity, compassion, and tenderness reside. We must also teach our daughters how to reach this place of restoration. Just as we have endured some things in life, so will our daughters, our granddaughters, and our great-granddaughters. We have to teach them that it is alright to cry sometimes. We have to teach them that the power of deliverance is in their tears.

When we cry, God heals us. When we weep and wail, He delivers us. God wants us to reconnect with our womanhood. When we cry, it allows God to soften and sensitize us in our hard places. Crying liberates us so that we can really be used for His Kingdom building on Earth.

When God called the weeping and the wailing women, they touched the hearts of those who lost loved ones. When we weep openly and publicly, God can use our tears to touch others, so that they, too, can feel and love again.

After you've had a good cry, the feelings of pain and defeat that once oppressed and destroyed your confidence and your self-esteem, will no longer have power over you. After you've had a good cry, you will be able to communicate in a new way. You will speak from a place of love and understanding, a place of patience and forgiveness, and a place of peace and joy. After you've had a good cry, you will know that you have received the victory.

Our "weeping may endure for a midnight," but our "joy will come in the morning" and we shall be restored after we've had "a good cry."

Reflections in Action

+ Get several pieces of note paper. Reach way down deep in prayer and ask God to bring everything that has caused you distress, destruction, hurt and pain to your remembrance and write those things down.

+ After you finish writing everything down, go get yourself some tissue.

+ Find a private place, get comfortable, read what you've written, and have yourself a good cry.

+ When the tears have ceased to flow, take the note paper, tear it into pieces, and throw all of that pain away.

+ Thank and praise the Lord for your deliverance, for you have been restored.

+ Remember, whenever you are hurting, allow yourself to have "a good cry" at the appropriate place and time.

+ Try not to revisit or rehash those things that God has already delivered you from.

+ Vow to the Lord that you will always be in touch with your emotions.

+ Don't ignore how you feel when you are hurting or you have been hurt.

+ Embrace the cleansing, healing, and restorative power of your tears.

+ Allow yourself to go through the process of healing so that you can be emotionally free.

Reflective Prayer

Father God,

I recognize that I have held back my tears when I really wanted and really need to cry. I come desiring to always be in touch with my feelings and emotions.

You created me to be a loving, sensitive, and caring woman. May I always respond to those things that touch my heart, so that you can use me to be a blessing to my loved ones and anyone that you have placed in my path.

God, thank you for the release and the ability to be used by you. When I feel hurt, I pray that I will respond and react in a way that makes a difference in your kingdom on earth.

God I desire to demonstrate your unconditional love in the way that I forgive others for hurting me.

May my tears spring forth from an inner fountain of love and joy. Thank you for the soul-refreshing experience of a good cry. In Jesus' name I pray.

Amen.

References &
Recommended Reading

Barclay, William. *The Daily Study Bible Series.* Westminster John Knox Press. 1975.

Clinton, Catherine. *Harriet Tubman: The Road to Freedom.* Back Bay Books. 2005.

Hine, Darlene Clark. *Black Women in America.* Oxford University Press. 2005.

Ingram, Jessica Kendall. *The Journey Inward.* Journey Press. 1996.

McDowell, Josh. *See Yourself as God Sees You.* Carol Stream, IL: Tyndale House Publishers, Inc. 1999.

Miller, Donald G. *The Layman's Bible Commentary.* John Knox Press. 1959

Tillich, Paul. *Dynamics of Faith.* New York, NY: HarperCollins Publishers Inc. 1958.

Vine. W.E. *Vine's Expository Dictionary of Old and New Testament Words Super Value Edition.* Nelson Reference. 1997

Warren, Rick. *The Purpose Driven Life: What on Earth Am I Here For?* Grand Rapids, MI: Zondervan. 2002.

Weems, Renita. *I Asked for Intimacy: Stories of Blessings, Betrayals, and Birthings.* Innisfree Press. 1993.